connective
selling

John Timperley

connective
selling

The Secrets of Winning 'Big Ticket' Sales

CAPSTONE

First published 2004 by
Capstone Publishing Limited (a Wiley Company)
The Atrium
Southern Gate
Chichester
West Sussex
PO19 8SQ
www.wileyeurope.com
Email (for orders and customer service enquires): cs-books@wiley.co.uk

Reprinted November 2004

CIP catalogue records for this book are available from the British Library and the US Library of Congress

ISBN 1–84112–612–8

Typeset in 11/15 Palatino by Sparks
http://www.sparks.co.uk

Printed and bound in Great Britain by TJ International Ltd, Padstow, Cornwall
This book is printed on acid-free paper responsibly manufactured from sustainable forestry in which at least two trees are planted for each one used for paper production.

Substantial discounts on bulk quantities of Capstone Books are available to corporations, professional associations and other organizations. For details telephone John Wiley & Sons on (+44) 1243-770441, fax (+44) 1243 770571 or email corporatedevelopment@wiley.co.uk

This book is dedicated to the four most important people in my life, my wife Joanne and my three daughters Melissa, Jessica and Hannah. Thanks for the love and the laughs – there's even more to come!

Contents

Acknowledgements

I am indebted to my very good friend Dr Ian Grace, for his research work into the attributes of great work winners and for many of the interviews – we got there in the end! I am grateful also to all of those who have attended my courses and provided the 'real life' insights into what works – and what doesn't – in today's world of selling. Thanks also to the acknowledged 'guru' of professional services marketing, David Maister, whose insights into buyer thinking have never been matched.

Finally, sincere thanks to all those professionals from around the world who have completed my questionnaires and given their valuable time to talk to Ian and me about the ways they win work. This book couldn't have been written without you (perhaps you may see yourself in here).

Introduction

The phone rang shortly after 2.00 pm on 23 January 2002. I had been expecting the call. A long-standing friend – an IT consultancy business development director – began to tell me the result of a £multimillion proposal that had taken weeks of his life and cost his business thousands in bidding costs. I had expected the news to be good. It wasn't.

My friend, the shock clearly evident in his voice, recounted the painful feedback he had just received from the IT director of a FTSE 100 company that had just bought his rival's IT systems renewal proposal. The IT director broke the news to my friend something like this … 'As you know, we were talking to you and a couple of your competitors about this tender. At the start of our discussions all of us here thought you were going to win – being market leader and all – and I suspect you were pretty confident too, given your track record in our sector.

'By the time you had presented to us you had been over-taken. The board were unanimous in their decision to go for someone else. I have my doubts that they are as good as you – but there's no doubt that you were outperformed and out-manoeuvred during the proposal process … basically, they nipped in when you weren't looking and beat you to the finish line.'

This book was born immediately after that phone call. You see, the truth was that I couldn't answer my friend's question, 'John, what *should* we have done to win?' I would simply have been guessing. Now, after researching what *really* wins big ticket work, I think I know. And the answers are here in these pages.

No matter how you dress it up, there are only three outcomes to a potential sales opportunity; either you will win it, lose it, or no decision is made and nothing happens! 'Connective Selling' will help you make the right move at the right time in the sales process and win more high value work.

> This book is based on what happens in the real world of selling in consulting and the wider professions. The ideas and techniques have been told to me, and used, during extensive research into what works – and what doesn't – when you meet your contact in the 'sales zone'.

Here's how I went about the task. I talked to and met with hundreds of senior professionals worldwide – people responsible for bringing in clients and selling products, services and ideas to them. I asked them how they did it, the challenges they face and how good they are at it. I also asked their customers and clients about their experiences of being 'sold to'. Then I developed a methodology that played to the strength of all good professionals – asking questions – an approach that would take them 'step by step' through the sale. It meant looking through their contact's eyes, and thinking the way buyers think.

I discovered that once you get 'into your contact's head', anyone can move easily, and with total integrity, through the sales process. There's no need for slick salesman's patter, half-truths, or fancy closing techniques.

I've called the approach 'Connective Selling' because people buy a product or service because it fulfils a combination of their needs and wants, AND they feel they can TRUST the person and organization supplying it. They are buying a RELATIONSHIP, one in which you need to demonstrate that you are *credible, capable*, and *compatible*. You form a mutual 'connection' during the sales process.

Why is succeeding in the 'sales zone' so important?
For most professionals it's becoming increasingly difficult to get a contact's time and attention – and even more difficult to turn it into a new business opportunity. These days you get fewer chances to get in front of a contact to impress because the traditional methods of marketing are losing their effectiveness. Here's why …

Direct mail response rates are declining because people are inundated with such correspondence. Most is seen as an irritation, and only very relevant items avoid the wastebasket. The legislation being introduced to counter unsolicited and 'spam' correspondence will only make it more difficult to reach individuals with direct mail marketing messages.

Voicemail has replaced secretaries as the efficient protector of senior people. Many executives complain of up to 20 sales calls a day. In the old days these would have been fielded by a secretary who only let through the ones who convinced them of their value to 'the boss'. Nowadays, if you are making the sales call, the best you can do is to leave a professional-sounding voicemail and hope that your contact returns your call. They very seldom do. Why? Because they probably have another 19 professional-sounding voicemails from people like you to answer too! And how long does it take to delete these? Just a few seconds.

Seminars, exhibitions and conferences are great for imparting information face-to-face and personal networking. However, as senior executives' available time becomes tighter, fewer are registering their attendance, and there are more 'no shows' than ever before.

Corporate entertaining and hospitality can, of course, be a fantastic way to build relationships and rapport. The problem is that some organizations have now banned their people from being indulged in this way by existing and prospective suppliers and advisers. They fear falling foul of corporate governance legislation and accusations of favouritism or underhand practices. Others haven't gone as far, but their senior executives find that they simply can't take significant time out of the business for non-productive activities. Yes, there will always be corporate hospitality, but there is a definite trend towards people being entertained less.

Advertising in the business-to-business world is also becoming tougher. A great advertisement still sells. But the challenge for advertisers is, which media to use? There's a multiplicity of national and regional newspapers, specialist and trade magazines, radio channels, digital and terrestrial television outlets and then, if that's not choice enough ... there's the Internet. The range of media channels is mind-boggling and, as a consequence, target audiences are split. Sometimes very small numbers are reading, listening, viewing or interacting with your advertising message. In short, its getting harder to reach the people you want to reach because of the sheer variety of media they could be using. As a result good prospective clients are harder to come by through these routes.

What's so different about this book?

To make it practical and easy to understand, we'll be following a 'route map' with an 8 Junction approach to selling without the 'hard sell', using proven techniques in the critical areas of:

- Building rapport and gaining a reputation as a 'Trusted Adviser'
- Writing and personally presenting work-winning proposals
- Negotiating a price that truly reflects the value you add

I want you to come with me on a journey through the 'sales zone'. Along the way we'll meet red and green lights, see the dangers of going too fast – and too slow; we'll hit potential roadblocks and diversions, and we'll experience the power of advance planning so that you know your next manoeuvre.

The 'journey' comparisons are sprinkled liberally throughout to enable you to relate immediately to the issues, based on your own driving experiences. By understanding the route a sale takes, and by taking the right action at the right time, you can massively increase your chances of reaching your intended destination – winning high value business.

CHAPTER 1

You are entering the 'sales zone' ...

What do you do when you have a contact who may be in the market for your product or service, and you've got the opportunity for a discussion with them – the outcome of which could be progress towards winning new business ... or an opportunity lost?

To increase significantly your chances of success in the 'sales zone' you've got to position yourself better than your competitors. This probably means changing the way you identify what your contact wants, understanding how they are motivated, and using approaches to the discussion that are designed to create a sense of urgency.

> Unless you are selling a commodity at the lowest price, you're selling value – a product or a service that allows your contact to make or save money, to solve a problem or improve their existing situation. However, just because you have something 'valuable' to offer, it doesn't mean that they will automatically jump at the chance. Your contact has to *want* to engage.

They may not 'see' the issue as you do, or recognize the value of the opportunity that you know is there; they might not think the benefits you can bring are worth all the effort involved. They may simply be apathetic to the opportunity you can provide.

That's why you have to have a methodology that engages them in a productive discussion – one that allows you to explore their needs and highlight how you can help.

As we go through the book we will identify, at each of the 8 Sales Junctions, the questions your contact is likely to be asking themselves, and the way you should be thinking and acting to maximize your chances of success. Where it's helpful I'll give you directions to tools you can use to plot your approach. I've also included throughout the book, comments from some of the great work winners I interviewed, sharing the routes they take to win new business.

That's not all. The 'Are you a Rainmaker?' self-test at the back of the book will allow you to pit your skills against these great work winners. Based on my research findings, it will give you immediate feedback on where you will benefit from learning new techniques because, as one senior consultant told me when I interviewed him,

> 'Selling is like racing model cars – if you spin off it's not the end of the world. You just start again with the added experience of what to avoid next time.'

Let's get going ...

SOME DEFINITIONS

Throughout this book you'll see references to contacts, buyers and decision makers. For clarity, I've defined them like this:

Contacts

A contact is the person who, for whatever reason, has asked you to have a 'Sales Zone' discussion with them. You may know them well, or not at all, but they are someone who can give you information about the organization and its needs if you ask the right questions and build rapport with them. They may, or may not, be a buyer or decision maker. They may need to pass the ultimate buying decision to someone else

---

higher or more relevant to your product or service. We'll meet different types of contact on our travels.

Buyers and decision makers

The way I've described them here, these terms are interchangeable. Buyers are the people whom you have identified as having the authority and budget to buy from you. We'll check out the different types of buyer later.

Decision makers are the same as buyers. However, in some sales there may be an all-important decision maker, e.g. the CEO or the owner of the business, whose decision is final, no matter what the other buyers say.

'Getting into the zone'

This book isn't about marketing and the things you do to get in front of a contact to discuss a new work opportunity. What it does contain, however, are a number of 'sound bytes' from my research that highlight some of the moves connectors make to help them get into the 'Sales Zone'. As you read, ask yourself, 'Do I do that ... if not, should I do it in future?'

'The buyer's view'

You'll see quotes from buyers that I gathered during my research throughout the book. The aim is to get you to focus on what the client is thinking at various points in the sales process. Do you recognize yourself in some of the comments? (Not all paint a beautiful picture!)

Taking the 'fast track'

I've highlighted what I think are some of the key points and 'must do' actions under the 'fast track' heading. Following these will, indeed, get you to your destination – a successful sale – more quickly and effectively.

Winning 'sound bytes'

The ideas and concepts in this book are based on what happens in the real world of selling in business-to-business, consulting and the wider professions. 'Winning sound bytes' at the end of each major section contains comments from some of those great work winners I talked to as part of my research. They shared with me some of the secrets of how they do it, the challenges they face and what results they achieve.

Whilst you are reading them, why not ask yourself these three questions:

■ Do I do this …
■ Could I do this …
■ Should I do this?

Succeeding in the 'sales zone'

An 8 Junction journey to winning high value work

We'll explore what we can do at each junction in the sale to understand what our contact wants and to put ourselves in the best place to win any potential work that may be available. We'll be breaking down the route into an easy to follow, logical journey.

Key questions to ask yourself

- Am I talking to the decision maker?
- Have I 'hit the spot' on the issues?
- Have I set out clearly why they should buy from us – and demonstrated what's in it for them?
- Do I know what my competitors are doing?
- Have I kept in contact enough – and in the right way?
- Have I generated enough urgency?
- Have I got the price right?
- Have I weighted the scales totally in my favour?

(flow)

Marketing → Contact → Proposition/meeting → Proposal/presentation → Result

Win/Loss

What happened?
- Don't want it
- Nothing
- Given to a competitor
- Not convinced of value
- Not sure of relationship (yet)
- OK in principle, but not now

What is your contact thinking?

- Am I the right person to agree this?
- Do I want/need this?
- What hassle will I have?
- What corporate/personal wins will this give me?
- Who do I need buy-in from?
- What would happen if I did nothing?
- Can I get it cheaper/better elsewhere?
- What results will I get and at what cost?
- What risks are involved?

Acknowledgement	Understanding	Acceptance	Respect	Trust	Bond

Figure 1.1 Succeeding in the 'Sales Zone'

CHAPTER 2

Winning new work through connective selling

Are you a 'connector'?

Those whose role involves convincing others to buy their products or services know how vital rapport building, listening and questioning skills are to their success. They also know that winning an assignment is all about understanding their contact's problems, seeing things from their point of view, identifying their priorities – and helping them to get what they want.

Creating new business in this way requires you to have a genuine interest in your contact's issues and opportunities, and a real willingness to 'step into their shoes' before proposing a solution that will work for them. These people are 'connectors'.

> At the heart of the connective selling approach lies one simple thing – understanding your contact's agenda.

This means:

- Focusing on the issues that really concern them
- Getting inside your contact's world to see things from their perspective
- Understanding each contact's needs (they will all be different)

- Identifying the challenges they are facing in pursuing their corporate and personal goals.

Your job is to develop a trusting and collaborative relationship. Connective selling requires you to be able to assess situations accurately, build long-term relationships and create mutual benefits. By selling in this way your contacts will see you as a true business partner – not just a supplier, but an integral part of their success.

GETTING INTO THE 'ZONE'

'He wouldn't call himself a great seller – it's not his style. What he is, however, is a great questioner and listener – and that's what makes him a great business winner. He really tries to understand the issues and become his contact's partner in the problem really quickly.'

What your contacts want ... and don't want

All of the research into selling shows that people have clear things that they want, and don't want, from their advisers and suppliers. What they *want* is evidence that you understand their sector, their business and their situation.

Once they trust you, your contact will look to you for help in:
- Clarifying their problem
- Identifying possible solutions
- Reassuring them that they are making the right decision
- Delivering the solution on time and on budget.

What they categorically don't want is:
- A hard sell
- To be told how to run their business
- Poor preparation
- Over-familiarity
- Passiveness.

WINNING 'SOUND BYTES'

- I've often wondered what prospective clients must think when advisers meet with them and ask basic questions about their organization, which reveal that they have taken no time at all to check out the various sources of information in the public domain. I know from my own perspective as a buyer that when this occurs I almost immediately 'write off' the seller as being not interested enough in my business. I research every prospective client before I go out to see them. It's not easy sometimes, but I can usually get the basic information very quickly – and impress just as quickly with my knowledge. It wins work, and gives you the credibility you need. (Actuary)

- One technique I use frequently is doing my prospective client a favour first – a small piece of free work, or introducing a contact who will be able to help them in their business. I do all this before talking about how I may be able to help them. I've found that they are much more receptive to me afterwards because, rightly or wrongly, they feel that they 'owe me one'. Some people may say that this is manipulative, but I'm not so sure. What I'm doing is trying to pave the way for a relationship where I've demonstrated that I am willing to help. If they give me something in return that's a bonus for me; I don't exert any pressure to do so. (Business development consultant)

- It's the little things that you do that set you apart as an adviser. The trick is to do things that others traditionally don't; for example, I always send an agenda a couple of days in advance of a meeting that not only sets out the points I would like to cover but also my goals for the meeting. I then follow it up with a call the day before to check if my contact has any additional points. I send any information that is needed for discussion in advance too. It avoids getting bogged down in the detail and leaves me more time for discussion of 'big picture' issues. (Lawyer)

- Instead of focusing organizations we would like to do business with, we concentrate instead on identifying the most influential business people in the markets in which we operate. It's then simply a case of building relationships with these 'movers and shakers', many of whom who have fingers in a lot of business 'pies'. (Engineering consultant)

- My one simple tip is to 'get out more'. Too many people do business these days by email and are more comfortable talking about what they are going to do rather than getting out and just doing it. I work on the principle that I will never sell my services by correspondence. Ultimately my prospective clients need to see the whites of my eyes and know that they can trust me to deliver. An email, letter or brochure can't create that level of trust. (Marketing consultant)

The decision to buy a product or service is based on personal as well as business needs. So, a crucial aspect of connective selling is to help your contact to see how choosing you will meet both their personal and their business agenda.

Experienced professionals know that they need to gain trust and build a bond of mutual respect with their contact, not only to make the sale, and repeat sales, but to make doing business with them a pleasure. How can *you* do it? The psychologists have a tool to help ... they call it the Relationship Triangle.

The simple framework that follows next explains how a relationship develops. It works for business relationships but as you read, reflect on your other relationships – you'll really see that the model applies there too.

CHAPTER 3

The power of forging strong relationships

The Relationship Triangle below shows how a relationship begins with acknowledgement, and progresses through to the higher levels when we like someone, and they like us, and we bond with them. That means we become friends and have real rapport and empathy with them. The strength of the relationship with your contact has a direct bearing on your likely success in selling to them. The higher up the triangle your relationship, the more likely you are to succeed.

Let's have a look why:

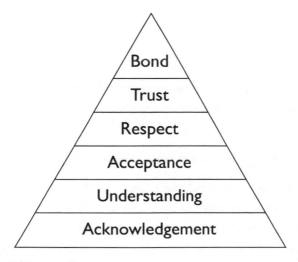

Figure 3.1 Relationship triangle

Acknowledgement

This is the basic start point of any relationship. If people don't know you it's very unlikely they are going to buy from you. That's why cold calling is so difficult, and mail shots to recipients you've never met generate such low returns. Acknowledgement is simply the stage where your contact knows your name. Perhaps you've met ... but do they *understand* what you do, and the benefits you can bring?

Understanding

If someone doesn't understand you, your products or your services you are not going to sell them anything unless you can show them that you can give them what they want and need. But understanding what you do and how you can help isn't enough either. They have to *accept* that you and your business are right for them.

Acceptance

Your contact has to accept you and your organization. They may know you, and understand what you do, but just not see your relevance to them. Indeed, they may not even like you! Either way, you fail the 'acceptance' test and there will be no sale here.

> **THE BUYER'S VIEW**
>
> 'I don't know you, I don't know your company, I don't know your product or service. Now what was it you were trying to sell to me ...'?

Respect

To make a sale you need the *respect* of decision makers. You earn it by having worked with them successfully in the past, or create it by demonstrating your knowledge, commitment and professionalism in the 'sales zone'. Existing relationships often make it a very uneven playing field when pitching for work against incumbent advisers, or others with whom your contact has a 'respect' relationship. But there are ways to redress the balance, as you'll see in these pages.

THE BUYER'S VIEW

'I really need convincing that you will deliver on your promises. It's my reputation that's on the line if you don't give me the results I'm seeking.'

Trust

If your contact *trusts* you to deliver, trusts your integrity and advice, and trusts that the price you are quoting is a fair one, you have a very good chance of winning the work – assuming that it adds real value to them and their business.

Bond

If you and your contact are at *'bond'* level, you've reached the pinnacle of the connective professional relationship. The decision on whether or not to use you or your organization goes much deeper than a business transaction. Emotional ties mean that, if all other factors have been addressed, you will get the assignment.

TAKING THE 'FAST TRACK'

What can you do in the 'sales zone' to raise your relationship with your contact to the highest level possible?

It's a good exercise to look at all of your existing client contacts and evaluate where you are on the relationship triangle. Then do the same for your prospective client contacts. The results will give you a 'snapshot' of your relationship status and a guide to what you need to do to get to the higher levels of respect, trust and bond.

> 'All clients are different! What suits one client will not necessarily suit another. The skill is in discerning which approach will work for each client. They will always appreciate the tailored attention such thinking generates.'

So says Sara Hopkins of Freshfields Bruckhaus Deringer in Hong Kong. Other connectors would agree wholeheartedly.

GETTING INTO THE 'ZONE'

'She didn't generate a lot of leads, most seemed to come from past clients who she kept in close touch with. But a great many of them gave us work simply because of the strength of relationship she had developed whilst working with them. They felt that they could really rely on her... there was a lot of trust and empathy there.'

Thom Singer of Andrews Kurth LLP, a US law firm, knows the power of forging strong relationships. This is what he told me during my research.

> 'Selling services is all about relationships. All things being equal, people do business with people they know and like. This means they must know and like you as an individual, and they must know and like the organisation you represent. Many people mistakenly think that experience and skill will always win.

> 'However, it is hard for some clients to distinguish between a good provider and a great provider, so they rely on "gut feelings". (Have you ever lost a piece of business to someone you know is not as experienced, but the client selected them anyway?) Therefore you need to

focus on quickly building rapport with your contact, so that you will stand out. There are no magic bullets on how to make that connection. Every situation is different, but if you focus on your contact and make them feel important to you personally, you will have success.'

WINNING 'SOUND BYTES'

■ I make it a priority to build some rapport with receptionists, secretaries and assistants who control assess to my contacts. It's a matter of being pleasant, getting them on side, asking for their help, taking an interest and generally recognizing the importance of their role. All of this, in my experience, helps to provide a platform where I am viewed as positive and supportive … and I'm sure that on several occasions I've got the work because they have put in a good word for me. (IT consultant)

■ We found that a great way to involve clients (and identify new work opportunities) is through joint brainstorming sessions. It gives us a chance to understand their business better and demonstrate that we know what we are talking about. Most sessions usually identify at least one way in which we can help them… and even if the brainstorming doesn't come up with anything new, we've built relationships and demonstrated our commitment to them. (Advertising agency)

■ To differentiate ourselves, we make sure that all our people's home telephone numbers are on the bottom of the emails we send. Our clients have commented that we show a real commitment to availability by doing so. Interestingly, our home numbers are very rarely called out of hours, as I think that clients naturally respect our home lives in the same way that they respect their own. As a result, we think we give a powerful message about commitment to being available without being a 'hostage to fortune!' (Lawyer)

■ Before a meeting with a significant new prospect I make sure we've read the industry magazines, talked to our clients in the sector about the big issues of the day, run a news search high-lighting their activities in the press and called their industry association for a review of what's happening. That's in addition to the stuff you would normally get from the annual report and accounts on the firm's website − remember that it tends to be largely promotional − and other advisers do that anyway. It's going the extra mile and checking out what the brokers are saying, for example, that impresses. I firmly believe that on occasions we've won the work after our first meeting with the potential client simply because we've done our homework effectively, and really demonstrated it to them in the meeting. (Corporate financier)

■ Our philosophy is to carefully select those organizations we want to do business with and really devote time to building rela-tionships with them. In our business winning new work doesn't take 5 minutes, so we devote real time to improving our knowl-edge of our contact's business and building our relationships with them. I guess you could say that we treat our prospective clients as existing clients − except we don't bill them! (Marketing consultant)

Nader Anise, a lawyer marketing consultant in the US, told me a great story about cementing business relationships. He believes that the biggest missed opportunity in professional services marketing is not acknowledging a new work referral properly. He said:

'I don't mean a simple "thank you" card or phone call. That's what novices do. Your appreciation for a referral should be expressed by something that is so personal and unique it makes the person want to go hunt down some more clients for you and deliver them to your door. The key is to acknowledge referrals in such a way that a) you make an immediate impact and impression, and b) the gift is memorable and keeps reminding the referring party of you constantly. The more you know about the referring party's likes, interests, hobbies, the better.'

Nader's company produces hi-end full colour lawyer cartoons that are personalized, based on the lawyer's area of practice. *'When my lawyer contacts receive them they are absolutely thrilled and display them proudly. They always think about the person that sent them,'* he says.

Another idea of Nader is to send a gift like a 'wine of the month.' *'I've purchased a magazine subscription for someone as a "thank you" before now. They think of me every time it arrives!'* he adds.

The overall message is that you have to acknowledge the referral immediately; do it in a big way and make it memorable for as long as possible. If someone sends you a referral once, it probably means they have more opportunities to send you the same type of client in the future. You just need to figure out what is the most memorable way to say 'thank you'.

Coming at relationship building from a slightly different angle, a former chairman of mine differentiated himself in the business world and, at the same time, created a huge network of business contacts by sending out personal handwritten notes to clients and other contacts every day. The fact that he had a very good 'copper plate' handwriting style with a fountain pen meant that his letters were seen as very personal and 'special'. In these days of word processors and emails, they are a refreshing change and he was remembered for them. Everyone likes to receive something that is personal to them. He found it a great 'door opener' and a platform for building longer-term rapport.

There is absolutely no doubt that the stronger your relationships with those in a position to give or refer work opportunities to you, the easier it will be for you to bring in new business. However, these days you can't just rely on your business or social relationships alone. You have to develop the skills and habits to ensure that when you are in the Sales Zone, you capitalize on the opportunity, not lose it – and that's what we'll cover next.

CHAPTER 4

Understanding and influencing your contacts

Now that you've got a feel for what happens between two people on the way to building a bond, let's focus on some of the vital knowledge you'll need to navigate the sales journey most effectively. Then I'll introduce you to the actions that effective 'connectors' take on the journey that makes them more successful than their 'average' colleagues.

Think back to when you first learned to drive. Your instructor taught you the fundamentals of how to do it and, until you got the hang of them, driving was probably a difficult and frustrating process. It's the same with selling – the fundamentals are critical to your success. They may feel awkward at first, but if you build them into your approach you progress much more smoothly and with less stress than if you just rely on what you think is right!

Connective selling is different to the 'ordinary' selling of products and services, because it's about taking a long term and relationship-focused view of doing business – to move from being just a provider of a product or service towards a genuinely 'equal partner' relationship.

The main differences look like this:

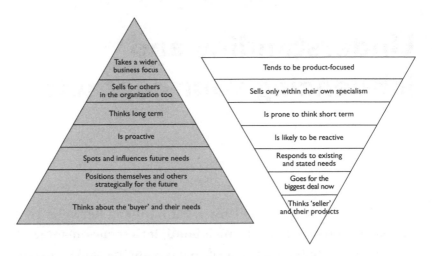

Figure 4.1 The Connector: The ordinary professional

Successful connectors put their contact first. They look at the sale through their contact's eyes and approach it from their perspective. They understand these fundamental principles of selling:

IS YOUR CONTACT A 'VISIONARY' OR A 'PAIN AVOIDER'?

We know that to sell ourselves and our product or service we have to *motivate* our contact to buy from us. However, the elements of motivation are not as straightforward as you may think. To take two extremes of the spectrum ...

> Some people are motivated by a ***vision of success***, whilst others are motivated by the ***fear of failure***. Your job as a connector is to discover what is likely to motivate your contact in any given situation.

It's not just about understanding what type of personality they are; it's about identifying what 'hot buttons' are going to be most appropriate to press on each occasion.

Some everyday practical examples illustrate the point that people doing the same things are motivated differently. Some of us exercise in a gym because we love the feeling that comes with physical exertion and pushing ourselves… we enjoy it; others exercise because they are frightened of getting fat, need to lose weight, want to maintain their health and good looks and are willing to go through the 'punishment' of it all. The exercise is the same but the motivation is vastly different. It's a similar comparison with holidays – some love holidays as a chance to go and see new places, spend time with the family and generally explore. Others take holidays because they need the mental and physical break away from work otherwise they will go mad! Everyone has their own motives for doing things.

Tom Freese, the great American sales trainer, tells a story that illustrates the point perfectly. Watching the 1996 Olympic Games, Tom heard Carl Lewis, one of the greatest track and field athletes ever, in an interview. Moments earlier Carl had just won the long jump gold medal on his final attempt. Amidst all the jubilation, he was asked by the interviewer, 'Carl, what was going through your mind just before you jumped?' As it turned out, Carl wasn't thinking about the medals, the money, the fame or the thrill of winning. Instead, he said that his primary motivation was that his family was in the stadium and he didn't want to *disappoint them* by losing his final Olympic event!

It's the same with many of your contacts in the Sales Zone. Instead of focusing on the benefits they can gain from your products or services, what they are really concentrating on is avoiding problems, issues or even failure by using what you are offering.

The key question for you is … what is your contact thinking, and how can you position your benefits appropriately?

It's not just a case of focusing on a vision of success. The majority of marketing messages, for example, tend to position benefits positively – that is, they appeal to the visionary side of 'this is what it will do for you, this is what you will gain, these are the advantages you will receive'. You now know that you also need to appeal to those who are motivated to seek relief from their present situation, solve problems, avoid issues and reduce their risk of failure. That means telling them how you can help in these specific circumstances too. Understand this and you are already ahead of many of your competitors in identifying what will motivate your contact to buy from you.

Why should they change what they've got?

Your contact isn't likely to do anything about their present situation unless they see a good reason to do so. When they do so, it's usually because they see a problem in staying as they are. So, the question for the connector early in the Sales Zone is: 'What problems or opportunities do they have that I can help with?' Even if you know, you are only halfway there. You also need to provide a convincing answer to a critical question in their mind: 'Why *should* I do something about it?'

Why should they choose you?

It's vital that your contact sees the consequences of not taking action. Clearly there is little point in talking about your product or services to a contact who hasn't yet decided they want to do anything about their situation. However, once they have accepted the need to do things differently, they then ask themselves, 'Is it worth considering you?' They weigh up what it will cost them. And 'cost' is more than just money. They also think about the time and hassle involved and consider any risks they may have. All of these make up the 'price' they will have to pay for your product or service.

Your job here is to help your contact to see the full value of your approach and show that the benefits of using you far outweigh any hassle and costs involved.

THE BUYER'S VIEW

'I'm sceptical about your proposition. I've seen and heard people like you before … why should I listen?'

TO SELL, YOU NEED A 'NEED'

Needs come in all shapes and sizes – big and small, personal and business, urgent and distant.

The best way to start understanding their perspective is to listen to what they have to say about it. You'll be able to tell a lot from the two different ways in which they talk to you.

If your contact talks about problems, difficulties, or dissatisfactions, and when they begin a sentence with 'I'm not happy with…', 'There's a problem with…', 'Our systems could be better…', they are expressing their *unconsidered needs*.

On the other hand, if your contact begins with statements like 'What I'm asking for is…', 'I need…', 'My objectives are to…', and 'It would help if…' they're describing their needs in terms of solutions, not problems. They are talking about what they want, not what's wrong. This is an *considered need*.

The distinction isn't a fancy theoretical one. Getting contacts to talk about their considered needs is strongly linked with successful sales. Unconsidered needs, on the other hand aren't. Just because someone is talking about their problems, doesn't mean that they automatically want to solve them!

THE BUYER'S VIEW

'I'm on my guard. Your proposition may imply that we haven't been doing it right up to now... and that could be my fault. I'm not sure that I would want that message to get out.'

Convincing your contact

There are three kinds of statement that sellers make to convince their contact – Features, Advantages and Benefits. You already use them automatically in your business conversations, but do you know the power and pitfalls of each? Let's take a quick review:

Features

A feature is a neutral statement about a characteristic of your product or service. For example: *'We have 250 people in our London office.'*

It's sometimes hard to avoid making feature statements, but the drawback is that they aren't very persuasive, so try to restrict them. Making too many, particularly if the sale is an expensive proposition, runs the risk of raising price worries in your contact's mind – especially if the features you mention aren't important to them!

Advantages

An advantage is a statement that highlights how your product or service will help. For example: 'We have 250 people in our London office, *which gives us specialist strength in depth in areas relevant to your business.'* It's an assessment by the seller of what they think their contact wants to hear.

Advantage statements are more persuasive than features, but, as a discussion progresses, their usefulness decreases rapidly. Why? Because the more you know the less you should be assuming things, or simply guessing. You should be working with what your contact has actually said that they want – their considered needs. The risk with advantage statements is that they can raise objections from your contact – often in the form of '… but I don't need that'. It makes a lot more sense to focus on their considered needs, which brings us to:

Benefits

A benefit shows how you can provide something that your contact has said they want. For example: 'We have 250 people in our London office, half of whom are specialists in the engineering sector *that you have told us is important to you.* **They are only 20 minutes away,** *which will meet your requirement for local experts who are readily available.'*

Benefits are easily the most powerful of the three types of statement, but sadly the least frequently used. At any stage of a discussion they are the most persuasive to your contacts; they are obviously relevant – because they have already told you what they want!

We learned in the introduction to this book that you need to demonstrate the 3 Cs of *credibility, competence and compatibility.* Trying to understand your contact's issues will help you do it; so too will identifying their needs and the options available to them. But the connector does more, much more.

They demonstrate their *credibility* through their generally confident demeanour, their initial impact and the way they deliver on their promises. They show their *competence* by highlighting how their knowledge and past experience can add value in this situation. And they demonstrate it in subtle ways too … in the questions they ask and the ideas they explore with their contact.

But the true connector recognizes that credibility and competence alone are not enough. They need *compatibility* with their contact – the 'chemistry' of two minds on the same wavelength, joined by mutual trust and respect. How do you forge such chemistry? Through listening and demonstrating genuine interest for a start; showing that you really do care about your contact's issues and opportunities and by going out of your way to help. Revealing your 'human side' is important too. No one wants to work with a 'know-it-all' automaton.

KEEPING IN 'ALIGNMENT'

You will probably remember a past discussion or two where the person you were talking to seemed to take a different – or sometimes completely opposite – point of view to you. Or, alternatively, when you've told a story, they've topped it with a better one! Sometimes it seems that whichever route you take you can't get your message across and, as a result, the conversation stalls.

Psychologists have a term for it – misalignment – and some people (annoyingly) habitually misalign what you say. It's an instinctive behaviour that causes people to 'push back' by taking a different view on what you've said. The habit is driven by the need to feel valuable and superior, and to add some value to the discussion. For example, if you said that the signs are that the economy is picking up, they would say that they haven't seen such evidence, or even that their feeling is it's getting worse!

People won't be contrary all the time, of course, but misalignment is more prevalent than you think – and as a connector you need to avoid it as much as possible. Why? Because disagreement, however mild, leads to resistance and, as a result, people tend to distance themselves emotionally to avoid further debate and the risk of confrontation. What you want is agreement, not disagreement. Misalignment reduces your probability of building relationships and winning work.

Watch out, too, for your own misalignment manoeuvres. In your eagerness to add value to the discussions you can easily find yourself injecting new views and information that can be seen by your contact as misaligning with them. Your contact doesn't want to be corrected, contradicted or made to feel smaller than you in any way. Stop yourself, or sooner or later you'll find yourself sitting on the hard shoulder in your 'sales journey'.

The good news is that it's easy to avoid misalignment once you know how. In connective selling, the more you push the more your contact will resist and push back. Sales trainer Tom Freese demonstrates this powerfully in his seminars. He asks for a volunteer from the audience then, standing facing him or her, Tom asks them to raise their hand as if they were taking an oath of office. He explains that this is a physical exercise and suggests that they might want to brace themselves so that they don't get knocked off balance.

Carefully, he places the palm of his hand against theirs and starts pushing – gradually at first. Then he increases the pressure until it is obvious to the rest of the audience that a significant amount of pressure is being used. How do Tom's volunteers react? You've guessed it, to a man or woman they push back harder and harder in response to being pushed. Remember, in this exercise the volunteer reacts instinctively to being pushed. It's the same in real life.

> If your contact feels that you are pushing them too hard, they usually respond by becoming unco-operative, unavailable, more cautious and reticent … and are generally more unlikely to listen to what you have to say.

What's the big point here? Well, it's simply that *telling is not selling*. Most of your contacts would buy from you if they were convinced of the real benefits of doing so; but they will resist being *told* to buy. They want to make the decision themselves. And that means that your job is to discover their needs and then, professionally and with dignity, help them to understand how you, your product or service can be of help.

Beware the silent misalignment gestures too

Remember, in business-to-business relationships your contact will sometimes disagree with what you have said (they'll misalign with you) but will keep quiet about it. They'll avoid confrontation in the discussion but will go away disagreeing with your statements or point of view. It's in this situation where you'll need to watch out for the body language that says, 'I don't agree with you.'

Defensive postures like folded arms and legs crossed away from you can indicate disagreement. So too can a host of eye movements and facial expressions. 'Steepled' hands or hands placed behind the head can also indicate that your contact has a different point of view.

A word of caution, however…

Reading body language is a complex area; you have to be alert to the implications of what you see … but don't jump to conclusions too quickly. Just because someone folds their arms whilst you are talking doesn't necessarily mean that they disagree with you – it could simply be that they are cold!

Watch for clusters of movement that MAY signal mismatching. If you suspect it, ask a question that seeks to clarify their view on what you have said.

Minimizing misalignment starts with prevention. If you habitually make statements when you are talking to your contacts you are risking misalignment. Almost any statement can be contradicted, clarified, bettered or misinterpreted in a negative (misaligned) way. Questions, on the other hand, can't. It's difficult to disagree with a question – and they also have the 'double-whammy' benefit of helping you to satisfy your contact's need to add value by providing the answer. They feel better – and you are still in agreement with them …it's a 'win-win' situation! *The message to take away is that, to minimize the risk of misalignment, you have to ask more questions and make fewer statements. It's as simple, and powerful, as that.*

WINNING 'SOUND BYTES'

- I started to get better at selling when I realized that it was a 'long game' and that I didn't need to 'close the sale' within the meeting, Now, I recognize that success can take many forms, each of which is building the relationship. I'm talking about gaining my contact's permission to bring in a specialist, to give me access to other key decision makers, or provide me with some business intelligence that will allow me to come back for a detailed meeting. Once the relationship is strong enough, the work normally follows. (Tax consultant)

- My added 'twist' to understanding a client's present situation on a specific aspect of their business is to ask how they are doing it now AND what led them to adopt that approach. The history leading up to the approach is generally instructive about the journey the organization has taken to get to this point. It leads to a natural dialogue about the results they have got and the gap between where they are now and where they would like to be. (Management consultant)

- I've never been trained formally in selling but I work on the old Dale Carnegie principle of winning my contacts over by talking about what *they* want and showing them how to get it! (Corporate financier)

- Over the years I have come to realize that, despite all the selling models and ways to sell, people essentially buy for their own very personal reasons. I see my job as finding out what those reasons are going to be. (Management consultant)

- Probably through nervousness, I used to talk too much in client meetings and try to convince the person in front of me that we

---

were right for the work. As I have become more experienced I have realized that the balance should be the other way round; if I get my contact talking about their situation and their business I know that I've got a chance; if I find that I'm talking about what we do, in detail, I know I'm falling into my old selling habits and am likely to walk away with nothing. (Merchant banker)

■ Whilst every selling situation varies, of course, finding out what the issue is, understanding the size of the problem or opportunity and identifying what my contact wants to do with it are all fundamental. I've got a series of questions that I'm comfortable with that are usually successful in teasing out information and give me the opportunity to act in a consultative rather than salesman role. (Business improvement specialist)

■ When I have successfully sold pieces of work in a single meeting it's always been where I've been able to take my contacts with me by focusing on areas of agreement, and by taking small steps at a time so that they agree with my train of thought. Some people call it building rapport and getting on the same wave length, but as I come from a scientific background I would like to think that there is some psychology in the fact that people have agreed with you up to a certain point and are reluctant to say 'no' afterwards unless they have a very good reason to do so. (Management consultant)

■ I like to create the right atmosphere for discussion by concentrating on their successes first – about what the organization and the individual is doing right and is proud of. Only then do I start to talk about areas where they might want to improve. In my experience this opens up the way for a much more relaxed conversation, as they have already demonstrated to me what they have achieved and how proud they are of their success. It gives a much stronger platform than immediately diving into problems. (Business improvement specialist)

The best way to demonstrate that you are eager to learn more and to show real interest in your contact and their business is to ask questions. Asking the right questions is more important in the Sales Zone than having the best answers. If you don't think so, then think about this. If you are going to sell a solution to a problem, or help them to capitalize on an opportunity, you need to know what your contact thinks the problem or opportunity actually is. And there's just no way to find out what your contact thinks unless you ask. Otherwise you'll just be guessing.

Let's delve a bit deeper into what type of questions actually work in building your image as a credible, competent and thoroughly likeable person.

GETTING INTO THE 'ZONE'

'My business comes largely from my personal contacts ... I pay a lot of attention to getting to know people. Not only that; so that I'm regularly at the front of their minds I go through my diary to check who I haven't seen in a while – then I call them. It's a basic but very effective discipline.'

CHAPTER 5

Questions – the key to identifying their issues and aspirations

If you are going to understand your contacts and help them to succeed you'll need information from them. To get it, you need to ask the right questions at the right time. In this section we'll first cover the seven vital questions that can guide the structure of any discussion in the sales zone. Then we'll focus on *what* questions to ask and *how* to ask them. But before you start ploughing ahead and firing out those questions, you have to gain your contact's permission to ask; it's both professional and consultative, and it avoids you being seen by your contact as some sort of interrogator.

Those you don't know well, or have met for the first time, won't thank you for bombarding them with your queries. You have to establish your credibility before they will open up to you. How do you do it without going into 'tell' mode (remember, 'telling is not selling'), and trying to convince your contact how great you are? The secret is to arouse their interest in what you have to offer, make them curious to find out more, and give you some of their time and attention.

IF YOU DON'T GET YOUR CONTACT'S INTEREST YOU WON'T SELL TO THEM

You've heard the saying 'You can lead a horse to water but you can't make it drink'. Connective selling is the same – there's no way that you can *make* your contact buy; rather, your job (metaphorically speaking) is to make them so *thirsty* that they *want* to drink!

> If you want to get your contact involved in a sales discussion you effectively have only two choices. Either you can try to force your way in by trying to convince them of your value (the 'tell' approach) or you can make them so intrigued by what you say that they want to know more ... in fact they'll invite you to tell them (the curiosity approach). Which method would you prefer – 'by invitation' or 'gatecrash'?

The first question I always ask a contact when we meet in the 'Sales Zone' is, 'Would you mind if I asked you a couple of questions?' Only one contact in a thousand will say 'no', and if they do you probably wouldn't want to work with these people anyway! Once you've gained permission to ask in this way you are off and running. There is, however, a real skill to asking questions that will position you as being better than your competitors, and at the same time help you to build rapport and credibility with your contact.

THE SEVEN VITAL QUESTIONS TO GUIDE YOUR SALES ZONE DISCUSSION

If you remember these seven questions you can't fail to structure your discussions with your contact effectively and come over as thoroughly professional and competent. What's more, there will be no 'hard sell' in your conversation whatsoever. Sound too good to be true? Remember this; if you don't know the answers to these questions then you will end up guessing what your contact wants or, even worse, assuming you know what they need. The task then, is a relatively simple one. In your discussions with your contact – over one meeting or several – you need the answers to these questions. Get them tattooed on your hand if you must, but remember them, because they are your route maps to success in the sales journey. Here goes…

1 What is your contact's problem or opportunity?
This isn't quite as obvious as it sounds. Your contact and the other key decision makers are all likely to each have a different perspective on their situation. They may see it a little, or a lot, differently. It's your job to get the 'big picture' not just one or two 'angles' on it.

2 Why do they see it as a problem or opportunity?
Find out the history of the issue or how the opportunity has originated, who is affected now and likely to be impacted in the future. Who says it's an issue or opportunity and what's the evidence for their view? Size it up – what's the issue costing them in terms of cash, time, resources, reputation etc? What could seizing the opportunity give them in terms of revenue, profile, efficiency, effectiveness etc? What's the size of the prize?

3 What do they see as a successful result?
What's their vision of success and how will they know when they have got there? In other words, how will they measure their results?

4 What are their major priorities?
They may have a number of priorities, but which do they see as most important? The answer tells you what matters most to them. Is it growing the top line, growing the bottom line, looking after their people, building market share, being more competitive, improving their operations, expansion or what? The answers they give will inform how you should position the ways you can help. Your message could be vastly different in each of the above cases … but if you don't know what their priorities are, and in which order they would rank them, you'll be guessing. You want to base your case around what matters most to the decision makers.

5 In what ways can you help?

You've heard the saying that 'there's more than one way to skin a cat'. It's the same here. To be truly connective in your sales approach you should set out the options for your contact and any other decision makers as you see them. Sometimes it means thinking laterally and collaborating with them on the pros and cons of each.

6 What results can they expect from each option?

Think through the results each of the options is likely to give them. Will the outcome match up to their expectations of a successful result (see question 3)?

7 Which do you believe is the best route to take?

Taking into account the answers to the six previous questions, what is your approach? It should be a logical extension of what you have said before, having weighed up what your contact and other decision makers want, and the best way you can help them solve an issue or capitalize on an opportunity.

Trying to persuade your contact to do anything without knowing the answers to these questions is like setting off on a 1000 mile journey to a destination you've never been before, without a map. Of course, you *may* get there, but it will be more by luck than planning.

Now we know the structure of the sales zone thinking, we'll get down to the 'nitty gritty' of, specifically, what questions to ask and when.

THE SCIENCE OF ASKING THE RIGHT QUESTION AT THE RIGHT TIME

Research by Huthwaite, the research and sales training consultancy, showed that the use of questions is *the* key selling skill.

The Huthwaite experts had heard so much about the merits of 'open' and 'closed' questions (the latter reducing the contact's answers to 'yes' or 'no', and the former allowing the buyer to answer in their own way allowing a longer response) that they expected this to be a crucial distinction. Not true! They couldn't find a link between the use of 'open' questions (which are usually claimed to be the 'good' kind) and successful sales.

'Open' or 'closed' questions were expected to 'open up' or 'close down' the other person's answer. But that's not how it happens in real life. In Huthwaite's research over 50% of 'closed' questions received long answers and over 50% of 'open'questions short ones!

That's not to say that the issue of using 'open' and 'closed' questions is irrelevant. Rather, the research didn't support the idea that the *form* of the question makes a difference; the *purpose* of the question is far more important.

Let's put the purpose of four types of question under the microscope. Each has its special place in the 'Sales Zone', but two in particular are the method of the champion connectors.

1 'Where are you now' questions

It makes sense to start with questions that are easy to ask and answer so that you can get the conversation moving. The connector uses 'where are you now' questions to gather background information and understand the context of the discussion. Wherever possible, though, they try to get some of the *basic* information in advance, from published sources, corporate literature, the Web etc to show that they have done their homework.

Typical 'where are you now' questions include:

- How many people do you employ?
- What products do you currently use?
- Who are your current advisers?

Use 'where are you now' questions early in the discussion to warm up proceedings. They are safe, easy to ask and require little planning. But watch out, because they can be overused. They mainly serve your information gathering purposes (your contact already knows the answers!) and can therefore make the discussion slow moving and boring from their point of view.

TOP TIPS FOR 'WHERE ARE YOU NOW' QUESTIONS

These questions are necessary, but keep them to a minimum, and with a definite purpose. Ask only those things you need to know. Spread the ones you have to ask throughout the discussions, rather than 'interrogating' them up front.

---

2 'What's the matter' questions

The purpose of these questions is to explore your contact's sources of dissatisfaction or worry, or to probe for opportunities they would like to exploit.

For example:

- What is your main difficulty with …?
- How happy are you with …?
- Do you see any problems in …?
- Where do you see the business in …?

'What's the matter'questions are more powerful than 'where are you now' questions because they involve your contact more and gain their interest. They can increase your credibility if you ask good ones.

TOP TIPS FOR 'WHAT'S THE MATTER' QUESTIONS

Plan them. There is no point in exploring problems or areas of opportunity that you can't help with.

By the same token, too narrow questioning can lead to missed sales opportunities by not discussing wider problems. Find a variety of ways of asking them too. For instance, there is a difference of nuance between 'What problems do you have with …?' and 'How happy are you with …'.

3 'What would happen if' questions

These develop and 'highlight' the problem or opportunity in your contact's mind by emphasising the positive or negative consequences.

For example:

- And what effect would that have on …?
- What might that lead to …?
- Does that mean that … is affected?
- Would that result in …?
- How would that improve …?

'What would happen if' questions are powerful but also the hardest to ask 'off the top of your head'.

TOP TIPS FOR 'WHAT WOULD HAPPEN IF' QUESTIONS

As they are hard to ask spontaneously, you'll need to plan them in advance. As well as thinking about what problems and opportunities your contact has, consider the consequences from their perspective so that you can work out a persuasive path of questioning. Try also to think of a *range* of possible implications: personal and business, external and internal, time, cost, business improvements and so on.

4 'What results do you want' questions

The purpose of these questions is to get your contact to think about the solutions they want, and benefits they'll get from solving their problems or capitalizing on their opportunities.

For example:

- What sort of approach are you looking for …?
- What do you see as the main benefits to you …?
- How important is …?
- Who else might be interested in this sort of solution?

'What results do you want' questions are great; particularly those that encourage your contact to explore *why* they want results.

TOP TIPS FOR 'WHAT RESULTS DO YOU WANT' QUESTIONS

Ask a variety, not just the 'do you want?' type. It's also worth planning for a wide range of possible success scenarios – including things that you might not currently know.

Check out the chapter on 'The connective way to win tenders' for many more questions you can use to demonstrate your capabilities and commerciality.

Now that we've explored the purpose of the four main types of question, let's get the inside track on some of the moves the best connectors make when engaging with their contacts in the 'sales zone'.

Some questioning 'tricks of the trade'
How to intrigue them …
How do you get your contact curious about what you are going to say next? The easiest way is to say, 'Can I ask you a question?' Almost without exception they will say 'yes' and start

wondering what you are going to ask them. And, as a result of your simple question, you have both their time and attention – it's the starting grid for the discussion and avoids you jumping straight into a series of questions without your contact's ok to do so. You could also make a statement that arouses their interest – something that gives your contact a 'sound byte' of relevant value such as:

- Our clients have saved thousands of pounds using this strategy and approach. Would you like to know how they went about it?
- If we could improve your operational efficiency by 30%, would you be interested in finding out more?
- The latest survey in the *Financial Times* indicated that many organizations in your industry are adopting outsourcing procedures just now. Our own experience with clients seems to back up this trend. Have you seen the survey results … would you be interested in our perspective on what's likely to happen over the next year?

Most of your contacts, all things being equal, would be sufficiently engaged by questions like these that they would want to continue the dialogue with you.

'This is new and you are one of the chosen few'
This approach works like this:

'We're just about to launch a new [product/service] that will save our clients significant sums of money in the area of [whatever]. *Would it make sense for me to give you a "snapshot" of how it works?'*

The idea here is that people like to be 'in the know' and, equally importantly, don't want to miss out on something that *might* be beneficial. Whatever their motivation, you can usually achieve your objective of engaging their interest.

'Everyone else is doing it'

This approach uses the 'herd' theory of 'If everyone else is doing it, should we consider it?' For example, 'A number of your competitors are taking steps to reduce their inventory and improve their time to market with the help of our software. Is this an issue for your business?'

This technique is one that arouses curiosity and raises a number of questions in your contact's mind.

To what extent is ...?

You want your contact to openly share what's important to them and why and, in particular, what their priorities are. One failsafe question for a connector to use in this situation is:

'To what extent is [whatever it is] important to you?' You can just fill in the blank with a relevant issue that helps to uncover needs and encourages your contact to expand on their responses.

Follow up questions include 'What about … Why is that important to you?', 'How important is …?' etc.

Tell me more...

It's vital to motivate your contact to keep talking when they are giving you valuable information. Use encouragers like:

What else?
Like what?
How did you feel about?
And then what?

Links like these give them a chance to keep talking and, at the same time, you demonstrate that you are interested in what they are saying.

Asking questions puts you in the driving seat in the sales zone and will direct every conversation you ever hold with your contact. Basically, the person who asks the questions has the power and control. They can alter the speed and direction of the discussion.

QUESTIONS GIVE YOU CREDIBILITY

> Questions that engage your contact's interest lead to you having credibility with them. They are a far cry from the 'tell' school of selling.

The questions you ask will help you to create the favourable impression you need on your sales journey. Your contacts will form their impressions quickly, based on your demeanour, what you say and how you say it. Such credibility is the key to your success in the sales zone; without it you won't be given access to key decision makers – and even if you do manage to get it, you won't be given the time and attention you need. On the other hand, the more credibility you have, the more comfortable your contacts will feel with you, which in turn will increase your likelihood of success.

TAKING THE 'FAST TRACK'

Memorize these questions and you'll never fail to make an impact on your contact. You'll probably need to adapt them for your own purposes, but the principles of identifying the big issues by asking professional, insightful questions are packed into each of these.

- How is your business structured now (how has this changed over the last couple of years)?
- How are you positioned in relation to your competitors?
- What initiatives have you in place to increase your competitiveness?
- What are the biggest pressures in your market just now?

- Are these likely to change over the next 3 to 5 years (and how do they compare with a year ago)?
- What are the challenges for you (and your business) in dealing with these pressures?
- What are your key business priorities for the next 6/12/24 months?
- What strategies are you using to achieve the results you are looking for?
- What impact will your strategies have on the size and shape of your organization?
- In the light of the strategy you've told me about, what are your priorities for [whatever is important to you]?

Add even more credibility ...

Asking adaptations of the above questions for your particular specialism will already set you apart from many of your competitors, but the great business winners – the best connectors – add something that allows them to impress even more. They preface their question with an observation that shows they know what they are talking about, and gives their contact some context for their answer. Compare the two approaches below to give you a feel for how they do it.

Connector...

'What do you see as the main issues impacting on your business today and in the near future?' (Great question, but a bit direct.)

This time the connector sets the scene first by making an observation *(in italics)* before asking the question.

Connector...

'*A number of our clients are finding that they have an increasing need to adapt to change – driven by competing products coming on to the market. That's one issue we're seeing* but I would be interested to know what you see as the main issues impacting on your business today.'

Here's another one:

Connector...
'What strategies are you using to deal with the present difficult market conditions?'

Set the scene by making an observation and you provide the reason for asking the question:

Connector...
'The computer industry has lived with slim margins on hardware for many years. Now it seems that software is also moving rapidly into becoming a commodity as well. What strategies are you using to deal with these difficult market conditions?'

Compared with ...?

> One of the ways to really get your contact interested in your dis-
> cussion is to include a **comparison** in your questions. There is an
> argument that if you ask the same questions as your competitors you
> won't be able to differentiate yourself from them. Your contact will
> simply observe that 'all you people ask the same things'.

And, what's worse, they will get *bored* answering the same question all the time. This is particularly true in competitive tender situations where all potential suppliers have the opportunity to interview the key decision makers to find out more about their requirements.

It must be a similar situation to the one celebrity film stars face when they have just launched a new movie. They move from city to city, country to country, talking to journalists and chat show hosts ... and get asked the same questions every time. How do they feel? *Bored!*

However, the great news is that you can keep your contact's interest with your questions – and indeed really make them think, by adding a *comparison* in some of your questions. And you get the added bonus that the answer you get back will give you some fresh information and insight that your competitors won't have – and that could be the difference between winning and losing the business. These examples illustrate this simple, but immensely powerful, technique.

TV interviewer ...
'Tell me about your latest movie ...'
Celebrity thinks ...
(I've answered this a thousand times already so I'll just switch on to autopilot and give the 'party line' ... brain disengages).

'Connective' TV interviewer...
'Tell me about your latest movie – *and how it compares with the others you've done over the last five years.'*
Celebrity thinks ...
(Hmm... I can't just give my usual stock answer here ... I'll have to think. In fact, how DOES this one compare with the others? Is it better, worse, different – and in what way? Why do I say that ... hmm ...brain engages).

It's easy to see the parallel for the questions you can ask your contact, and how much more information you can potentially get out of the discussion. What's more, your contact will think you are really sharp and insightful. What answers would *you* give to these comparison questions, picked from the 'fast track' panel earlier?

- What are the biggest pressures in your market just now ... *compared with three years ago?*
- What do you see as your key business priorities now ... *and in what ways have they changed over the last two years?*
- What major strategies are you adopting to win new business ... *and how do they compare with the strategies of your competitors?*
- You've told me that your business is growing at 20% a year *... how does that compare with your competitors and the market as a whole?*

Each of these questions, if you have taken the time to consider them properly, should have made you stop and think. You just can't answer them by rote, and 'off the top of your head'. They need thought and consideration. The connector who asks incisive questions like these, in a relaxed and non-intrusive way, leaves their contact thinking that they have had a very stimulating, interesting and thought-provoking discussion. And that's exactly the impression you want to leave them with. Simple technique; really powerful result.

TURNING THE SPOTLIGHT ON YOU

One of the easiest ways to change the focus of the conversation onto your offering without over pushing is to ask, 'Would it be valuable for me to tell you about how we can help with [whatever issues or opportunities you have discovered]?' Asking in this way avoids 'misalignment' (see earlier) and gives your contact the chance to give you the 'green' or 'red' light to go ahead and tell them.

If you get green, you know that you are on the right road and your contact is interested. On the other hand, if you get a 'red light' when your contact declines your offer to tell them more about you and your products or services, they've given you some fantastic feedback that something has gone wrong somewhere in your questioning. Maybe you jumped the gun and are trying to present your solution before you've identified the right issues. Maybe they don't see the situation as you see it, or maybe you haven't gained their confidence yet. Whatever the reason, it's your chance to clarify their views and check your position in the sales zone. You've not skidded off the sales road yet but, because you've asked their view on what should happen next, you've merely slowed right down and are continuing with caution until you get the signal to go on.

The connector's way to check for green and red lights

> There's no need for any salesman's fancy closing techniques. However, what you DO want is to be sure that you have your contact's commitment to move forward, and agreement on the appropriate way to do it.

And you need to do all this in a way that is professional and courteous and avoids the possibility of 'misalignment'. How do you do it? By making a statement and *asking a question*, the answer to which will give you a real indication as to their level of commitment to the next step. If they are at all hesitant to put some of their own time and effort into doing what you suggest, watch out – you have at best an amber light. Listen to the way they answer the question, and watch the body language. Act accordingly.

Connector…
'Can I suggest that I give what we've discussed some thought and present some options to you in a week from now? Does that timing suit you?'

Connector…
'We certainly have the resources locally to do the work for you. So that we can assess the scale of the project properly it would

be very helpful if you could let me have a specification for the assignment and I'll come back to you with a costing. Is that alright?'

Connector...
'I understand that you need to involve others in the decision. I'd be very happy to explain the options to your colleagues at another meeting. Do you feel that this is the best way to move forward?'

Connector...
'Thanks for a very interesting discussion. I think you're right in suggesting that this is a decision for your colleague. If, as you suggested, you have a word with her and I call later in the week to set up an appointment, would that be alright?'

Connector...
'I agree that some one-to-one meetings with your senior colleagues are needed so that I can understand the scope of the work properly. Should I get my free diary dates to your secretary so that she can match them with their availability?'

Connector...
'I think we both agree that there are a number of options possible. I'd like to develop a discussion document and personally present it to your board for discussion at next week's meeting. Are you agreeable to that?'

Connector...
'As we discussed, project management is not my area of interest. If it is OK with you, can I get my colleague John Brown to give you a call to pick up the issues you mentioned and explore how we may be able to help?'

WINNING 'SOUND BYTES'

- I aim to understand my contacts' problems as soon as I can by trying to feel what it's like to be in their position dealing with the situation at hand. It's a really good way to get on the same 'wavelength' and explore what could or should be done. (Lawyer)

- I don't think I've ever 'sold' anything to anyone! My technique is to find out where we can help people get to where they really want to be in the areas that are important to them and their business. (Accountant)

- Some of our best marketing is simply done by asking clients what they like and dislike about our service, and how we performed on our last assignment. But you need to do this face-to-face, not through a questionnaire. The honesty in asking for such feedback often leads to identifying other ways in which we can help – particularly if the feedback on our previous work is very positive. (Lawyer)

- In my experience no one wants a generic solution; everyone thinks they are different! That means you've got to give them real proof that your solution is tailored to their specific situation. That means asking some real in-depth questions about their particular situation. Of course, when I'm talking about how we can help, I refer to other clients where we have done similar work, but I'm at pains to point out that my contact's situation is different in small but significant ways, and I recognize that these need to be addressed. Such an approach immediately moves me away from the 'one size fits all' danger. (IT systems provider)

- Rather than 'second guess' people and get into selling mode, if I think we've got an opportunity for a piece of work or the chance to introduce someone else from our business I just come out and ask my contact if it 'would be of value to … (whatever it is)'. People generally give me an honest answer. So, if it is of value, people will say so and we agree on a course of action. If not, I know that I should either explore their reasons more deeply (sometimes they have not thought it through), or recognize that now is not the right time to do it. (Tax adviser)

■ We've won work many times simply by demonstrating that we've really tried to understand our potential client's business. Sometimes we have had our research people do a comparative analysis with their competitors to give them fresh insights into their standing and provide some helpful discussion points. Then we structure our discussions with the client around asking questions about how they view the findings ... we get in dialogue mode on issues rather than selling mode. (Management consultant)

THE BUYER'S VIEW

'Don't tell me you can solve my problems before you have understood my situation and my business. Ask good questions – and listen to my answers – don't try to "sell" me by telling me all about you.'

There you have it. These are the fundamental principles of selling in a professional and consultative manner by understanding what your contact needs or wants and asking thoughtful, insightful questions. The driving parallel is obvious. Without a sound knowledge of the basics – what to do and what not to do – there's no way you will become a competent driver. So it is in the 'Sales Zone' – if you don't know how to act and what to do when, you're in for a bumpy ride in attempting to win new work!

Let's hit the road in earnest now. Using a logical and easy to follow sales 'route map', we'll be passing 8 Junctions on the way to our destination – winning new business. Each junction has an introduction designed to 'set the scene' and let you know what's ahead. It highlights what your contact will be thinking, and the moves you should be taking to keep ahead of your competition and make effective progress.

CHAPTER 6

Navigating your way round your contact's head ...

JUNCTION ONE

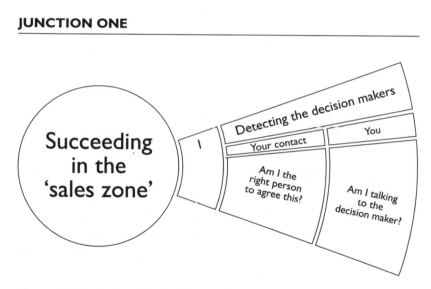

Figure 6.1 Detecting the decision makers

As soon as your contact has got a sense of what you are offering they'll be thinking, ' Is this stuff relevant to me – and am I the right person to agree this?' And, although it's very early days in the discussion, it's vital for you that the answer is 'yes' otherwise your sale will be stalled before you've even got going.

There are two sides to this road, however, because whilst you are making your introductory 'pitch' you need to assure yourself that you are genuinely talking to a decision maker – someone who can say 'yes' to you.

> To avoid wasting your time you need comfort that your contact is the person who makes the decisions or, at the very least, can give you access to those who can.

In these days of complex organizations and corporate structures not everyone you speak to will be the 'head honcho' who has ultimate say in whether to appoint you, but you need to know their role in the sale and the power and influence they have.

Not everyone can give you the green light, but many can give you the red light for their own personal reasons. You can be certain, however, that anyone who doesn't understand the benefits you, your product or service can give them will ultimately put up the STOP sign. That's why its vital for you to know who decision makers really are so that you can understand their issues and perspective and they, in turn, can give you the green light to carry on.

A study by Johnson and Bonoma found that there was an average of seven corporate decision makers for major product purchases, and five for 'big ticket' services. The point is, your contact is probably only one of a handful of people who need to say 'yes' before you win the business. And, if you don't know who else is in the buying team, you're likely to be beaten to it by a smarter competitor – or your proposal could get lost in internal 'red tape' as your contact struggles to get 'buy in' from others.

The reason for this is simple – when multiple players are involved in the buying decision it's more difficult to secure the consensus needed to get the green light to appoint you. Each person forms their own impressions about you and what you offer, and while some people will favour you, others may support someone else. Some may even prefer the status quo of no change because that's the easiest decision to take. That means that your proposition must be successful in bringing all these people together to make a decision in your favour.

But we're putting the trailer slightly before the vehicle here. What you fundamentally want to know before you get any further is ... 'Is working with this business going to be good for me?' Do I actually want to set off on this journey in the first place? And is it going to be worth it when I get there?!

The head of a corporate finance boutique I interviewed put it well. He said:

> 'If we haven't already got a relationship with a prospective client, the chances of us winning a competitive pitch situation are really low, unless there is an exceptional reason why they would choose us. As a result we often choose not to bid – it's probably saved us many thousands of pounds over the years. Where we **do** have established contacts in an organization and are competing with others, we go 'hell for leather' in ensuring that we meet with them to really get under the skin of their issues and understand the type of help they are looking for. We believe we win far more than our fair share of business in these 'head-to-head' situations simply because we've been selective'.

Ask anyone who runs a business whether *all* of their clients have integrity, are hassle-free, pay on time and are profitable. You shouldn't be surprised if their answer is 'no'! You can lower the odds of collecting trouble-causing and loss-making clients by asking yourself the eight 'qualification' questions at Junction One. In doing so, you'll also have made an initial 'gut feel' assessment of your chances of making a sale by looking at the nature of the business, the decision maker contacts you (and your competitors) have, and what their attitude is to price, service and delivery.

Kamila Havel from Hewlett Packard in the Czech Republic puts it like this:

> 'Never be afraid to turn down an invitation to tender if you don't think the client is going to be a good profitable prospect for you. Once you have a short (and it should be short) list of who you are going to pursue, every effort can then be made, resulting in a far more direct and focused line of attack. They may not have any work for you immediately, but if you ensure that you maintain the dialogue with them, you will be in the front of their mind when they do need to call on someone for assistance.'

This quick 'Go/No Go' procedure is the equivalent of checking your oil, tyres and vehicle and asking yourself, 'Am I really ready for this trip?' No one wants to end up on the hard shoulder halfway into the journey. In the Sales Zone there's no one to rescue you – you're on your own.

If you want to do your 'preparatory checks' properly, use the go/no go tool – there's a template on page 177 in Chapter 13 to help you make your decision. Let's say your 'check' comes up 'green for go', what next? Now you need to assess who is really likely to make the decision, and how they may help (or hinder) your progress. Will they be your coach, sponsor or even anti-sponsor? You'll find the full 'identikit' profiles on page 180 in Chapter 13, but just to give you the highlights of whom you could meet on your sales journey, consider this:

Coaches

They support you and want you to succeed. They have credibility and influence with the buyers, and you have credibility with them. Indeed, a good coach can tell you who the really powerful decision makers are, what's in the budget, what your competition is up to and help you get on the 'inside track'. They are like the parking attendant who guides you to the free spot in the crowded car park!

Sponsors

They support you and want you to be selected, usually because they see their own interests being served by a decision to choose you. The best sponsors have influence in the decision-making process. Through what they say and do they can significantly impact on how you are seen by other decision makers and give you a head start in the sales process. (Don't be smug though, your competitors may also have a sponsor.)

Anti-sponsors

These are the 'traffic cops' of the sales process as far as you are concerned. For their own reasons (maybe good ones) they want to catch you out. Watch out, they are likely to be there somewhere ...

> **TAKING THE 'FAST TRACK'**
>
> Think about your last sale. Can you label any of the contacts involved as coaches, sponsors and anti-sponsors?

If you can identify your coaches, sponsors and anti-sponsors, great, but that's only half of the story. Next you need to think about what TYPES of buyer those people assessing your product or service are likely to be. They fall into three main categories:

Economic buyers

Usually responsible for 'bottom line' impact on their organization and as a result focus on value for money and return on investment. They have the power to give the green or red light to the sale.

User buyers

They tend to look at what's in it for them; and no wonder, since they will be 'using' the products/service you are selling. If it really impacts on their role and responsibilities you can bet that they will judge you well, or harshly, in relation to any competitor's offering. You need to carry them with you.

Technical buyers

They do 'just what it says on the tin' by judging the technical aspects of your sales pitch. Your skills, qualifications and experience and those of your business will be scrutinized, compared and measured against what their organization has specified. Beware, you can get a permanent 'red light' if you fall foul of the technical buyer decision maker.

> ### THE BUYER'S VIEW
> 'Gain my confidence by demonstrating that you understand my situation and issues, not by telling me what I should do.'

The table on page 179 in Chapter 13 gives more detail on how you can 'spot' the type of buyer you'll be meeting on your next sales journey.

Let's put it all together now, and check out what your contact is likely to be thinking at Sales Junction One. Then we'll consider the questions you should ask and the actions you could take.

For a start, you need to know the decision-making process; who will be involved, who the budget holder is, and who will have the final 'say' in going ahead? Only when you know this stuff will you be in a position to consider your chances of success.

However, it's not easy to ask your contact outright if they are a 'decision maker'. First, it's bad manners to suggest that you doubt they have the power to appoint you. Second, you are unlikely to get a straight answer anyway! One recent study asked a range of people involved in a sale who would ultimately make the decision – they all said it was them!

You need a more sophisticated line of questioning, one that will keep your fledgling relationship intact. It's at this stage that the great connectors probe for who the decision makers are, and the process they will go through by asking a question like, 'Who else should I speak to about this?' Such a question gives their contact the opportunity to consider who else would have a say in any decision, and needs to be convinced of the value of what you are offering.

Once you know who the decision makers are, you can gain your contact's permission to speak to them to get their views (and at the same time you can start to assess *their* relative power in this sale).

TAKING THE 'FAST TRACK'

Assuming you've done your research properly at Junction One of the sale, you'll have worked out who the 'players' are, and how much 'say' each is likely to have in the decision. If you've talked to them you'll know what is important to each in relation to your product or service and assessed whether they are likely to be for or against you.

Last, but by no means least, your go/no go tool will have given you a good feel for whether this potential piece of business will be good for you.

On your sales journey you'll now be motoring along nicely, and starting to get a clearer view of how to navigate what lies ahead.

GETTING INTO THE 'ZONE'

'When I hear about a potential piece of business I call around my contacts to see if someone can make an introduction to the buyer for me. It still amazes me how many times I can find someone who knows them. Believe me, it's much better than a cold call when I say that a mutual contact has recommended I speak to them – I get an invaluable measure of credibility straight away.'

Junction One: detecting the decision makers

What is your contact thinking? Am I the right person to agree this?

Your key questions and actions

Key question	Am I talking to a decision maker?
Ask them:	Who else should I speak to about this?'
Test yourself:	Who will make the decision to go ahead? Contact all relevant decision makers (with permission) and assess the power of each in the decision-making process.
Act:	Consider who could be your coach, sponsor or anti-sponsor and why (page 180).

Make a go/no go profile and decide if you should invest time in the opportunity (Chapter 13 page 177).

1. What do they want/need?
What's your impression of their requirements?

2. What do they do?
What sector? Is it one you're familiar with?

3. Who's in charge?
Who are the decision makers?
Who has the power and control?

4. What's on their agenda?
What are their plans?
Check on their annual report, company literature, web, trade press, etc.

5. Who do you know?
Your past work (if any) and success or otherwise.
Who do you know and how well? Will they be for or against you?

6. Who do your competitors know?
Are they likely to be better placed than you?

7. What's likely to be the winning price?
Your pricing history with the potential client (if any).
Your strategies in recent sales compared to your competitors

8. Is working with them likely to cause you any problems?
Are they financially sound? Will they pay your bills?
Potential conflicts of interest?

GETTING INTO THE 'ZONE'

'One of the best things I do – and I don't know too many who do the same – is that I make a point of meeting not only the decision makers on an assignment, but their more junior colleagues too. They are flattered for one thing, and tend to support you more, but the real payoff is when they get promoted or move on – and they bring me and my services along with them. It's the most cost-effective marketing I could do, and all it takes is time and appreciation of people.'

JUNCTION TWO

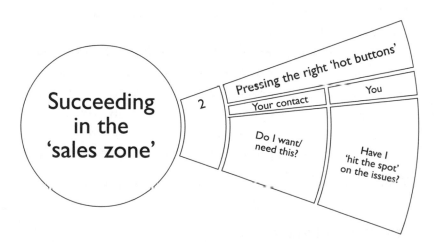

Figure 6.2 Pressing the right 'hot buttons'

Having heard your proposition at Junction One your contacts will now be asking themselves the next big question, 'Do I want or need this?' To sell your product or service you have to convince them that it will add real value to their business and that it is much more than an optional 'nice to have'. You can only be successful if you understand your contact and their organization and, as a result, can categorically demonstrate that you are offering exactly what they need. It means really 'hitting the spot' on the important issues.

Passing this Junction successfully is not about guessing, or assuming you know what they want; it's about asking the right questions to uncover their corporate and personal challenges, hopes and expectations.

> You can be sure that individual decision makers will have different perceptions of the most important priorities and needs … to continue your sales journey you need to understand them all.

Use the Decision Maker's Analysis Tool in Chapter 13 (page 181) to help you to capture their issues, and assess how you can give them what they want.

Your goal as you travel further into the 'sales zone' is to get to a point where you know (because you've probed, not guessed) what the 'big issues' are in the area of the business relevant to your offering, and thought through how you can help. Remember, there are both corporate and personal 'agendas' going on here. Capture them so that you are aware of all the 'avenues' you'll need to explore.

THE BUYER'S VIEW

'Show your sensitivity to my issues. I'm not the same as everyone else, so recognize that fact when you talk to me.'

Now for the bad news. Exciting though it is to identify what you think are the major business and individual 'hot buttons', you are only at the starting line. Your challenge now is to introduce these into your further discussions with the decision makers to test how 'hot' they really are.

Junction Two: pressing the right 'hot buttons'

What is your contact thinking? Do I want/need this?

Your key questions and actions

Key question	Have I 'hit the spot' on the key issues?
Ask them:	'What challenges does your organization and sector face at the moment, and what are your priorities just now?'
Test yourself:	Do you know the business' top 5 issues and opportunities?
Act:	• Assess how you (and others within your organization) can help the business, and individual contacts. • Use the 'Decision Maker's Analysis' (Chapter 13, page 181) to capture the issues for each. Assess how you have met/will meet their needs. • Try these for starters: • What is each of your contacts trying to achieve (in their job or in their longer term career)? • How can you help them meet their goals (corporate and personal)? • What kind of approach do they want or need? (The answers to these two parts may differ.) • How do they deal with their existing supplier/adviser?

GETTING INTO THE 'ZONE'

'When she has a good idea to save them money with a new consulting angle she approaches all her clients with it, systematically. She's the best I know at selling new products to existing clients, simply because she works out the benefits, and then, after understanding their issues, tailors her 'story' for each client. She soon generates some great case studies of successful application … which makes her even more convincing.'

THE BUYER'S VIEW

'Really listen to what we want – don't just give me your packaged solutions and hope they fit.'

JUNCTION THREE

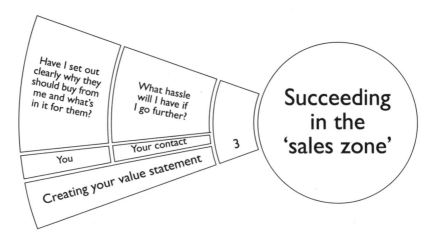

Figure 6.3 Creating your value statement

Now that you have demonstrated the relevance of your product or service, your contact will be getting round to musing on the potential 'hassle' they may encounter should they take discussions further. To counteract their tendency to think that all of this may be too much trouble, you need to be crystal clear about what you are offering and the value you will bring.

Your contact's 'hassle' may simply take the form of the time they need to devote to the discussions, or the administration and paperwork resulting from a change of adviser or supplier.

> Whatever constitutes 'hassle' in their eyes, you need to convince your contact that taking you on will be a positive and smooth process with the minimum possible disruption to them and their business.

They also need comfort that you will deliver, and not leave them personally and corporately exposed as a result of engaging you.

On our sales journey this is a big 'traffic light' Junction. If you don't convince them it's worthwhile continuing you'll get the 'red light' and the sale will be stopped. Maybe they will still be unsure, in which case you'll encounter slowing down tactics – 'amber lights' that allow your contact to maintain control. What you really want, of course, is a 'green light' that says, 'Go on, I'm interested in taking this further and I'm willing to put some effort into making it happen.'

That means demonstrating the *value* of what's in it for them, and setting out clearly why they should buy from you. Your offer needs to bring together all the arguments necessary to convince each buyer to choose you rather than your competitors. A *'Value Statement'* highlights why a buyer would want to buy something from you – and sets out clearly what's in it for them. Creating a convincing one is not as easy as it sounds. Bad ones tend to have one or more of the following weaknesses. Test your own sales messages against them:

Is your Value Statement...?

- Too generic (can it be applied to other businesses or situations easily without adaptation?)
- Full of features, without benefits (see page 24)
- Not specific to your buyer type (see page 57)
- Not tested with your decision makers (how do you *know* that what you are proposing is what they want?)
- Similar to one that your competition will come up with (in which case why would the decision makers choose you?)

The converse of these points are, of course, the mark of a good Value Statement. When you've captured it on paper, take a minute to check it against these simple tests:

- Is it clear?
- Does it address the decision makers' needs?
- Can you deliver it?
- Can you prove it?
- Does it differentiate you?
- Is there real value in it for the client?
- Is there value in it for you? (Will what you propose be profitable?)

You may have a single 'Value Statement' for a sale or, on some occasions, multiple value statements. It depends on what the decision makers want, what type of buyer they are and their attitude towards you and your product or service. The key to success is to make your Value Statements *specific* to them so that you become memorable for your approach, particularly where there is competition around. (We'll see what your competition may be doing when we meet them at the next junction.)

Richard Oakes, the global marketing director of Eversheds, the law firm, focuses his people heavily on creating value statements. He told me: 'In my view, unless you can succinctly articulate why your contact should choose you, you can't hope to be in control of winning the business. It's about controlling the persuasion process by creating a crystal clear value statement where the only logical decision your contact should make is "yes, we need you".'

THE BUYER'S VIEW

'Convince me that you have something of real value to offer, not just promises that you will deliver.'

Use the Value Statement Tool in Chapter 13 page 184 to help you think through your sales messages. Consider what you can do right now to demonstrate your credibility and professionalism. It's about taking action that will give the decision makers comfort that choosing you will be the right move. You need that 'green light'. Have a look at some of the ideas in the Junction Three action summary over the page.

GETTING INTO THE 'ZONE'

'We use tailored seminars to help us find prospects. Simply by the fact that they have registered to attend, we know that they have some interest in the issues and therefore may be in a position to buy from us. The secret of our success is not in the event itself – although that has to be professional – it is in the follow up afterwards. We phone them, not to 'hard sell' but to get their views and see how we may be able to help. We get a dialogue going, and some of those conversations turn into new work down the line.'

Junction Three: creating your value proposition

What is your contact thinking? What hassle will I have if I go further?

Your key questions and actions

Key question   Have I set out clearly why they should buy from me and demonstrated what's in it for them?

Ask them:
- 'Are you happy that we have covered all of the issues important to you?'

Test yourself:
- Are you looking at a red, amber or green light just now?
- Do I really know and understand the criteria on which I am being judged? If the answer is no, try to find out before presenting your solution, otherwise you may as well be shooting in the dark.
- What is my value statement? (That is, the package of reasons why individual buyers should choose you.) Your offer should bring together all the individual statements necessary to convince each buyer to choose you rather than your competitors. The statement shouldn't simply state your capabilities, but show how you could help individual decision makers and contribute to the company's success.

Act:
- Complete the Chapter 13 Value Statement (page 184) and Decision Maker Analysis (page 181) tools.
- Check them against key messages you have already given in meetings, your general communication, written documents and any oral presentations. Do you need to do more? Use all contact opportunities to demonstrate your efficiency and effectiveness, and the value you bring.
- Send agendas and CVs in advance of meetings.
- Write within a day of meetings.
- Test your propositions through all meetings with decision makers and decide which are most important.
- Show how your product/service will make things better for your contacts.
- Demonstrate how your offer is better than your competitors.

> **THE BUYER'S VIEW**
>
> 'I won't believe what you say until you provide me with real proof that you can do it – and convince me that you have done it successfully before.'

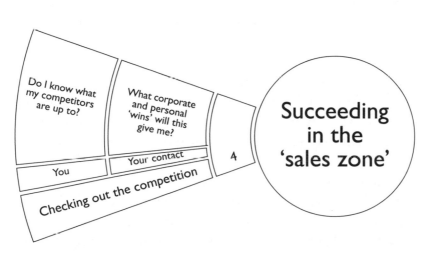

JUNCTION FOUR

Figure 6.4 Checking out the competition

Whilst they may not articulate it, at this stage on the sales journey your contact will be assessing what you can help them to do, from both a business and a personal standpoint. They want to know what corporate and personal 'wins' they will get ... and this usually leads to comparing you with your competitors or alternative solutions.

All drivers have had the unnerving experience of checking their rear view mirror and seeing an open road behind them, only to be overtaken seconds later by a fast-moving vehicle. It's the same in sales. You need to know where your competitors are so that you don't end up blocked behind them or are, metaphorically, forced off the road by someone who has generated some real sales momentum.

You may not be alone on an open sales road, despite what your contact tells you. Now's the time to check if your competitors are already ahead – and glance behind to see if they are likely to be coming up fast.

> Not all sales situations are competitive, but even on those occasions where there's not a competitor in sight (you think …), it's worth considering what they would do if they were in your position.

You may be called upon to demonstrate to your contact that if they go with you they'll definitely get the biggest personal and corporate 'wins' – and that means thinking through your advantages over your competitors in this *specific* situation.

Stuart Dey of UK accountancy practice AGN Shipley makes sure his firm remembers that his contacts have choices. 'It's all too easy to forget your competitors when pitching for new work – you get so focused on your own message. We've learned to lift our heads up and consider what our competitors will be saying to our contact. It gives us a new perspective – and momentum to deal with a competitor's challenge.'

If you've already got competition on the scene, now's the time for some serious concentration on the road ahead, focusing on who's pitching and how they are going about it, who they know and who they are getting to know; whether they've won work here before and what their sales 'pitch' and price is likely to be.

THE BUYER'S VIEW

'You need to make it clear how much you want the work, and why you are better than the others talking to us. If you don't, why should I give it to you?'

Use the Competitor Mapping Tool on page 183 in Chapter 13 to help you. You need to know what your competitors are up to, so ask your contacts directly. Some will give you a straight answer, others won't. Your coaches and sponsors (Chapter 13, page 180) may know the answers.

After analyzing your competition, now's the time to prove you have something to offer that your competitor can't match – even if it's only enthusiasm and a 'hunger' to win the work. Have a look at the actions you can take to understand your competitors' positions, and what you can do about them in the Junction Four action summary.

Junction Four: checking out the competition

What is your contact thinking? What corporate/personal 'wins' will this give me?

Your key questions and actions

Key question Do I know what my competitors are up to? Are they ahead or behind?

Ask them: 'How are our competitors approaching the proposal?'

Test yourself: Is there anything else we should be doing at this stage to neutralize our competitors' advantages and highlight their weaknesses?

Act:
- Complete the Competitor Map (Chapter 13, page 183)
- Who is pitching? Style of approach?
- Who do they know?
- Have they worked with the decision makers before?
- What was the result?
- Any potential conflicts of interest for your competitor?
- Competitors' expertise/USPs/products & services/ likely sales approach?
- Prove you have something to offer that the competition can't match.

GETTING INTO THE 'ZONE'

'He always sees opportunity in every situation. Other people can see fifty reasons why something wouldn't work, but he can see fifty reasons why it would. He's what I call a "practical optimist" and his attitude is important to his success. He just keeps on moving forward, despite setbacks …and he's won business simply because his contacts like the way he thinks. They know that if he is working for them he will give it 100%.'

JUNCTION FIVE

As we saw at Junction One (above) it's unusual for a major corporate buying decision to be in the hands of one person (although there are exceptions). Your contact will usually need to get 'buy in' from others. They'll be considering which colleagues they need to convince that the initiative, and you, are worthy of support. So before they start touting your solu-

Figure 6.5 Maintaining momentum

tion round their organization and singing your praises, they'll need to be sure that you really want the business – and are capable of delivering.

The sales journey parallel is about keeping your 'foot on the gas' in order to make steady, consistent progress. It's about avoiding losing concentration and, in effect, pulling off the road into a lay-by for a lengthy snooze. It involves keeping the momentum of the discussions and communication going, and making a positive impression at every contact opportunity. That means treating your contact like a prestige client and maintaining regular, welcomed, dialogue.

> There will have been many instances where a sales opportunity has 'gone cold' because either you or your contact, after the initial spell of enthusiasm early in the sale, has lost interest or hit a 'road block' of some sort. It may simply be that other issues have become more pressing for your contact and you have fallen from 'front of mind' onto the 'back burner'.

To maintain that 'front of mind' position without being seen as too 'pushy' requires real connective sales professionalism.

Remember the whole premise of connective selling is that you and your client want the same thing – a solution that truly meets their needs – and it's with this in mind that you are doing them a favour by keeping the issue high on their agenda because you know it is important to them. Having this as your intention takes away any guilt you may have of being perceived as pestering your contact. Indeed, taking the thought to its logical conclusion, if you do less than your best to maintain the momentum of the sale you are letting your contact down by failing to help them get what they want.

This isn't fancy philosophy, it's sound business sense. We've all been in a position where we were considering buying something but decided to 'think it over' and then let the excitement slip away and the urge to buy was gone. However, had the right salesperson come along at the right time you would have bought. A good example that applies to many people is the sales letter that interests you, but is never followed up by a call that would clinch the sale for the sender.

'There is no "silver bullet" to winning work,' says Deborah Scaringi of US-based Adler Pollock & Sheehan P.C. 'Set contact goals and then do everything in your power to continually move towards them from several coordinated angles. It's this conglomeration of efforts that ultimately brings in the business. These may include personal visits to gauge service and needs, contact entertainment, speaking engagements or seminars, clippings from newspapers regarding their industries and so on. Whatever the angles are, I believe you can't win business with just one effort.'

THE BUYER'S VIEW

'If you want me to sell the idea to my colleagues you had better give me good material. Tell me why we should do it and why with you, in a way that is succinct, otherwise I'll be a poor salesman for you.'

It's vital that you keep the dialogue going. There is some sales folklore that it takes on average six separate approaches to a contact before a sale ensues, but most salespeople give up well before the sixth contact. Your programme to maintain momentum with your contact has to be sophisticated and relevant so that you maintain credibility and demonstrate that you have their interests – not yours – at heart. It may take six contacts or more but if these are relevant, and add value to them, your contact won't mind.

TAKING THE 'FAST TRACK'

Have a go at preparing for your next meeting or telephone call using the Meeting Planning Tools on page 185, Chapter 13. The example Contact Planner on page 186 of Chapter 13 will also give you some good ideas on keeping the momentum going. So too will the Junction Five action summary below.

Junction Five: maintaining momentum

What is your contact thinking? Who do I need buy-in from?

Your key questions and actions

Key question	Have I kept in contact enough, and in the right way?
Ask them:	'How do you want us to keep in touch with you throughout this process?'
Test yourself:	Have I shown that 'working with us' will be better than with a competitor?
Act:	Keep your foot on the 'gas'. Try these sales accelerators:

- Treat every decision maker like a prestigious client contact.
- Prepare fully, and send material in advance of meetings to each decision maker. Complete the Meetings Planner (Chapter 13, page 185).
- Look for the opportunity to generate further contact after each meeting.
- Invite clients into the office and 'roll out the red carpet'.
- Write within a day of any meeting. Show you have listened and responded.
- Offer a 'brainstorming' session or presentation.
- Create an opportunity for a small assignment to demonstrate your capability, if appropriate.
- Consider use of all relevant media – email, letters, telephone or face-to-face – to produce a tailored communications programme. Think about wider personal contact – corporate hospitality/dinners/ social events.

THE BUYER'S VIEW

'Everything you do as part of the sales process will be noted by me, consciously or subliminally. You need to stand out from the crowd in the way you communicate with me and the other decision makers.'

GETTING INTO THE 'ZONE'

'He's very focused, and some days he'll spend a full eight hours just renewing contact with people on the phone. No hard pressure selling, just saying "hello" and finding out what people are up to. It's surprising what he finds out, and how many opportunities arise – not always straight away, but over the next few weeks, as a result of reminding people about him.'

JUNCTION SIX

Accelerating the sale by generating urgency in the mind of the decision makers is one of your critical success factors. If there's no rush to do something, most people tend to put it off

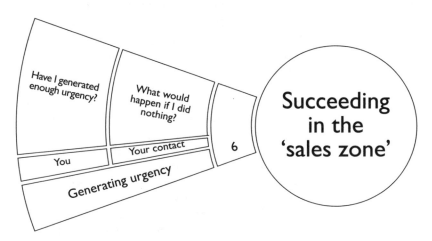

Figure 6.6 Generating urgency

– and often never get round to doing anything about it. A lack of urgency can bring the 'kiss of death' to the potential assignment; your contacts recognize the value ... but don't want to do anything about it at the moment. The task at this Junction is to show that it is to your contact's significant advantage to take action NOW.

You need to create that sense of urgency. Why? Because urgency encourages people to take action when their problems are painful enough or the opportunities you have described are exciting enough for them to do something about them. In many ways connective selling hinges on this point, turning a contact who is lukewarm to what you are offering into one who wants to use you, your products and services. You can increase your contact's sense of urgency either by offering some new information and insights or by asking questions that will help them discover opportunities to improve their existing situation. Urgency works. People with a sense of urgency want to get on with it ... and that's alright by you, because it means new business.

At this Junction your contact is likely to be asking themselves, 'What would happen if I did nothing?' If the answer to this question is 'not much' or even 'nothing', you'll have to work really hard to win the potential work.

You need to do this by emphasizing the business and personal benefits of taking action immediately, as opposed to later. This means thinking through, and articulating, the implications of a delay and the negative impact on the business/decision maker if they choose to do nothing.

THE BUYER'S VIEW

'Are these people really going to make a difference? I've got plenty of other issues on my agenda already ... maybe I should defer any action for the time being until things get a bit quieter.'

The great connective sellers are masters at focusing their contacts' minds on making a decision. They'll have got a 'feel' for how urgent the project is by asking questions like ... 'When do you want the work to begin?' ... 'How quickly do you want to see some results?' or ...'When do you want your people to start using the product?' It's here where you can hit a sales 'dead end' or the equivalent of a seller's traffic jam. You want to progress but you are just going nowhere. It's frustrating, but there's not much you can do about it until you convince your contact that staying where they are will cause them big problems. Once they see the need to do something the sales road opens up again. But how do you do it?

The aim is not to push your product or service on to them through fancy closing manoeuvres. Rather, it is to put yourself in their shoes and to help them get what they want by showing them the benefits of taking prompt action. They need to convince themselves of the urgency required.

THE BUYER'S VIEW

'I'm a bit worried ... will your approach really work as well as you say? Have you told me all the downside if it went wrong? Why should I do it now, as opposed to waiting?'

It's a fine line, but your *intention* is what counts. If your mindset is geared towards helping your contact move on the project quickly because it is in *their* interests to do so, then it will come over in what you say and do. Equally, if your attitude is a self-serving one, and your intent is to get them to make a decision because it makes your figures look good, you can bet that it will be telegraphed to them overtly in your behaviour, or subliminally in your body language and tone of voice. Remember, connective selling is about creating a win–win result for both of you.

Junction Six: generating urgency

What is your contact thinking? What would happen if I did nothing?

Your key questions and actions

Key question   Have I generated enough urgency?

Ask them: 'When do you want work to begin on the assignment?'

Test yourself: Is there likely to be a sales 'traffic jam' ahead, which could bring the discussions to a halt?

Act:
- When will the decision to go ahead be made?
- Have I really set out why the assignment is important, and the implications of not taking action?
- Highlight the negative impact on the business/buyer if they did nothing.
- Focus on the personal and business benefits of taking action now.

GETTING INTO THE 'ZONE'

'I send lots of "thank you" cards to people. Not only does it make people feel good for the work they've given to me or the contacts they've helped me to make, it also brings in referrals. Many a time I've got a call from a contact who has just received a "thank you" card, to say that a colleague of theirs may be in the market for my services too. I'm not sure of the psychology behind it but I think it's probably something to do with people saying "thanks" for treating me as special. Whatever it is, it works!'

JUNCTION SEVEN

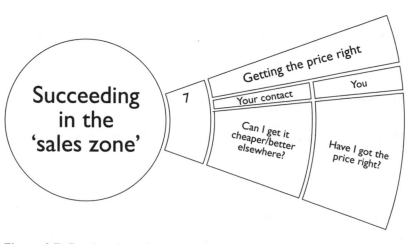

Figure 6.7 Getting the price right

Now we've arrived at what many sellers see as the 'crunch' Junction. You can bet that at some time during this stage of the sales journey the thought 'Can I get it cheaper or better elsewhere?' will drift gently across your contact's mind. At the same time your own thoughts are focused on 'What is the right price for my product/service?', 'What do they expect for their money?' and 'What will my competition be charging?'

Sometimes the answers to these questions are no better than guesswork and, what's more, having travelled so far in the sale it's easy to lose your nerve and start paring your price down in the hope of getting the figure 'right'. True connectors have a different and altogether more lucrative approach.

> You need to convince potential buyers that you are the right person (or organization) for the job, and that price should not be the deciding factor – unless, of course, you are likely to be the cheapest. This means emphasizing other selling points such as experience, specialism, availability, strength-in-depth, sector knowledge, resources, past history of success etc.

This is about comparing your offering with others, highlighting relevant features, advantages and benefits and showing that you will give greater value for money. It's what happens when you are buying a new car. If price were the only factor in the purchase, everyone would be trundling round in the cheapest vehicle. But there are hundreds of makes and models on the road – because they meet the specific needs of those who bought them. Your price needs to do the same, to reflect what your buyers want and highlight what's in it for them by choosing you.

A strong relationship – at Trust/Bond level – (remember the Relationship Triangle at the beginning of Chapter 3, on page 11) often makes the price question have less importance, or even go away, because your contact TRUSTS that the prices you quote are fair and competitive. That's the power of a strong relationship. However, if you are not at Trust/Bond level your challenge is to demonstrate that your prices/fees represent real value for money and show commitment on your part.

TAKING THE 'FAST TRACK'

Check out over the page some of the many pricing options and permutations you can use without simply lowering your prices. Which are you using now – and which, with a bit of creativity, could you apply to your business?

Anna Bialkowska of legal practice Denison Till in the UK has an interesting 'angle' for those who are shy about discussing their pricing structures.

'Having worked in commercial firms for 17 years prior to coming into the professional sector, one of the curious things I have noticed is the embarrassment factor that comes up sometimes with regard to pricing.

'My advice is to be as transparent as possible,' she says. 'Commercial organizations are not embarrassed about discussing pricing, and appreciate openness – they have budgets and bosses to keep happy. Imagine yourself in their position – you would probably want to have a very good idea of costs and would want to know immediately if there are likely to be any increases and why.'

A few thoughts to get your pricing 'creative juices' going
Don't be bald – get measurable!

Whatever you do, don't just put a 'bald' figure in your proposal without any justification or explanation. You have to set out how the decision makers will gain from your product or service and, where possible, show how your approach will bring measurable improvements, savings or improve their 'bottom line'. In other words you need to explain what they will get for their money and demonstrate that they will obtain significantly more in terms of results than they pay for your product or service.

Offer 'freebies' ... then put a value on them

To demonstrate your commitment to the potential client, and show your commercialism, consider offering some aspects of your product or service free of charge – but if you do, make sure that you put a value on them so that the decision makers know that you are giving them something of real financial benefit. You can also value the 'start-up' costs you will incur when you win the assignment. This shows that it is costing you a significant sum to get set up to help them – costs that you are willing to absorb for their benefit.

Put your money where your mouth is ... and take on all the risk

Potential clients are increasingly demanding that suppliers share the risk on projects. Think about the possibility of gaining competitive advantage by offering contingent or success-related fees. So, for example, if your service is designed to save money or measurably improve efficiencies, you get paid according to how much you save the organization or how efficient and effective they become as a result of your work.

There's always the classic 'risk free' approach that lends itself to some industries and professions.

Dare **you** say, 'If you are not completely satisfied with the results we obtain (benefits we give you/your product) you may have your money back, no questions asked'?

It doesn't suit all situations or organizations, but where it does fit, it's a powerful demonstration of your commitment to the potential client – and a show of your confidence in delivering exactly what you promise. In other words it could be a real differentiator. No matter whether your price is significantly higher than your competitors, if the decision makers know that you are so committed to getting results for them that you are willing to take all the risk, they should take you very seriously.

Compare what they've had with what they'll get
You need to emphasize the difference you will make. If you are cheaper than their existing supplier say so, and highlight why. If you are more expensive, say so – and highlight the significant product or service benefits they will get from you – benefits that far outweigh the difference in price. It's about justifying any price movements, up or down, so that your price is both credible and supported by facts that the decision makers agree make sense. Show your contacts that they are getting value for money and a 'good deal' from you.

Fix a 'ceiling'
Potential clients hate the thought of writing an 'open cheque' for products and services. They fear taking you on and then

opening the floodgates to additional costs and fees as a result of your work. Allay their fears and calm their nerves by offering a fixed price, no matter what happens; phase assignments so that they know what they are paying for each stage, or offer a fixed fee for a particular period of time.

Get on the 'inside lane'

What you really need is some inside information on what the winning price is likely to be. Of course, if your coaches and sponsors have been as good as you hoped, they may have given you a good 'steer' on what the 'ball park' figure may be, and what your competitors may be charging. One of the tactics of the champion connectors, however, is to informally 'test' the price with one or more of the decision makers who are favourable to them. Not all will agree, but if they do, you are reasonably sure that they will give you an honest view on the competitiveness of your price in relation to your opposition – and whether it is in line with their expectations.

Leave the door open

Leaving room for negotiation is probably the most important point of all for complex products or services, difficult-to-price assignments – or simply a piece of work you don't want to lose. Make sure that you put a caveat in your pricing to say that you would not wish to lose the work on price alone and that you would welcome a further discussion on fees/price should the way you have costed the work mean that the decision makers are likely to choose an alternative supplier of products or services.

As experienced connectors will testify, this is a 'double-edged sword'. On the one hand it shows that you are willing to negotiate and you want the work. On the other, some would argue that you immediately weaken your bargaining position by demonstrating that you are willing to 'move' on your price (see page 133 for the issues). Only you will know whether it is better for you to show flexibility, or to demonstrate that you believe you have costed the job accurately and fairly in your price and are going to stick to it.

THE BUYER'S VIEW

'Your prices were the same, but your competitors offered us payment options that made it more advantageous for us to buy from them. It swung the balance!'

There are many ways of looking at price. Much depends on your own circumstances and the industries/sectors in which you operate. The basic idea is to be creative in your pricing, to justify what you are charging by saying what the client will get for their money and, wherever possible, taking some of the risk yourself. In this way you make their decision to choose you so much easier. On top of this, if you can find out the price the decision makers at your potential client are expecting to pay, you are well on your way to winning the work.

GETTING INTO THE 'ZONE'

'She always goes in with a low price first on a small project so that the client can get a taste for her approach. Nine times out of ten, they are so blown away by the results that they soon want her to do more. Because she's built the relationship and proved herself, asking for the full rate, and more, for the next assignment is never an issue – they know she will deliver value for money.

'Another way she gets in the door is to offer an "it will cost you nothing if we don't get results" approach. She seems to be taking on all the risk if it doesn't work, but she knows that her service can save clients' money in almost every case. She often gets bigger fees this way by working on a percentage of the savings as her reward for a successful outcome.'

Junction Seven: getting the price right

What is your contact thinking? Can I get it cheaper/better elsewhere?

Your key questions and actions

Key question   Have I got the price right?

Understanding the value of your proposition can help you support the fees you quote. (See 'Nearly there ... the art of negotiating profitable terms', Chapter 11, page 151).

Ask them: • 'How important is price in your decision?'

Test yourself: • How will the decision makers gain from your product/service?
• How will your ideas bring savings or improve the bottom line?

Consider these actions:

Act: • How much are the savings/improvements worth?
• How will they enhance shareholder or corporate value?
• Check competitors' likely tactics. Are you in the 'ball park' on fees?
• Test your fees/price informally with the key decision makers before submitting
• Put a monetary value on any 'freebies' you are offering, and value your start-up costs if appropriate
• Offer a 'taster' at a low price
• Phase assignments
• Offer fixed rate fees or for a fixed period
• Consider contingent or success-related pricing
• Compare to previous service levels
• Benchmark against similar assignments
• Justify any fee movements up or down
• Show the impact of any efficiencies you bring
• Leave scope for negotiation

JUNCTION EIGHT

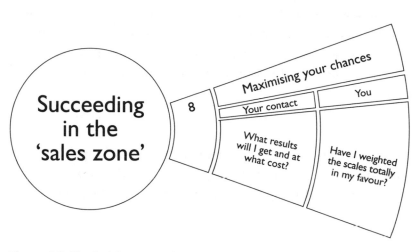

Figure 6.8 Maximising your chances

Now your contact is getting edgy. They've gone through the sales process, asked you the tricky questions, tested your commitment and professionalism and, where appropriate, compared you with your competition. You've given them your price and value statement, and they will have to make a red or green light decision soon – that's why they tend to ask themselves again, 'What results will I *really* get, and at what cost?' (And remember, the 'cost' is more than just the price, it includes the 'hassle' of taking you on.)

Your contact may be worried about a number of real or perceived risks in engaging you and giving the 'green light' to the assignment. These include:

- Choosing the wrong supplier
- Spoiling their own reputation
- Disrupting the business
- Upsetting colleagues
- Wasting their money

You need to be **explicit** in highlighting what results and benefits your contact will get for their money, and prove why these will be worth the effort and cost involved. Further, in what you do and say, you need to build that TRUST between you and your contact so that the perceived benefits of a successful project far outweigh the potential risks.

There are a number of techniques you can employ at this Junction to give your contact further confidence in you and what you are offering. Try building some of these into your repertoire:

Give them great references
The great thing about references is that they can boost your credibility by showing your contact that what you are proposing has worked for someone else. That puts your contact's mind at rest, reduces their perceived risk and paves the way for a discussion on how you may be able to help them. References can also be great for arousing your contact's interest in you and, specifically, what you have done for others like them.

Reduce their risk
Your contact wants to minimize the risk of anything going wrong in choosing you. Sure, if they make a good decision and you deliver on your promises they will get a corporate 'pat on the back' (who knows, maybe even a promotion). If they get it wrong, however, they may be in deep trouble, their career progress may be hampered, their department – or maybe the entire business – could be affected. Making decisions can be serious stuff, with big implications. It's natural then, that your contact will want as much comfort as possible that they are making the right move. That's why references from others are an important crutch for them to fall back on.

The problem with references, however, is that everyone uses them. Showing how you have helped ABC company is good, but unless ABC's situation is exactly the same as your contact's business you are entering a 'misalignment' minefield.

There's another problem too. Almost anyone can produce a list of happy clients (unless they are really bad or a 'start-up'). Your contacts know this and are usually suspicious of pre-prepared client references. After all, you are hardly likely to include someone who really hates you in your list of referees!

The clever way of using references is to avoid individual testimonials or case studies unless they are absolutely relevant to your contact, and even then back them up with the 'herd theory' – a technique that surrounds your contact with a sense of momentum and the comfort that they are doing the right thing. The idea is to show that lots of other businesses like them are already interested in what you offer. Once you've shown that 'important others' are moving in a particular direction it's much easier for you to motivate your contacts to do the same. Psychologists have proved that people are strongly influenced by the thoughts of important others – as long as there are enough of them. There's something in the comfort that safety in numbers brings, coupled with not wanting to miss out on the benefits everyone else is getting. Your contacts also see that they can have the benefit of learning valuable lessons from those who have already undertaken similar projects or bought the same products.

Know your clients intimately
No, I'm not talking about getting to know your client's issues in depth – although that's vital if you want to succeed in retaining them, adding value and winning further new work. In this case I want you to focus on your client list – your personal list and that of your wider business. Most people, when asked to name their clients of a particular size, in a specific geographical area or sector, can mention four or five (or maybe a few more) and

then get stuck. The ace connector, however, demonstrates their confidence and credibility by rattling off an impressively long list of relevant clients when asked.

Test yourself: How many clients can you name, without pausing, in a particular geography, industry or turnover band? After you've had a go, assess how many you **could** have named if you had your business' client list handy.

The more relevant clients you can name the more you will appear to your contact as being on top of your business. If you feel you've got room for improvement, keep practising by reviewing a specific category each day for a week. You'll soon absorb the information and be ready for any questions like, 'Who else do you work with in our sector?', 'Which other businesses in our city do you advise?', 'Give me some examples of organizations of similar size to us that you are involved with.'

Whilst this is all very clever, and far more effective than drying up after four or five names and saying, 'I'll get back to you with other names after I've researched who we have in your [sector/city/size band],' it's only the starting gate for the really impressive manoeuvre.

After reeling off an impressively long list without hesitation, you then say, 'If you would like to contact *any* of the organizations I've just mentioned for their view on our services I'll be happy to arrange it.'

Then, when asked, you are able to give a named contact and job title for each of the ones requested, together with a bit of detail about how you have helped them. The true connectors can even give individual telephone numbers! Such a move shows that you are in regular, committed contact with your clients. But you don't have to be a memory champion to achieve this feat. You will already know the core of the list where you are personally involved with the client. For others, where you are not directly involved, simply stick a piece of paper containing the key contact, job title and telephone details of your organization's major clients in the front of your notebook or diary and glance at it as necessary as a aide-mémoire.

> Successfully negotiating this critical Junction means asking yourself what else you can do to 'weight the scales' totally in your favour. It's about reviewing all you have done so far in assessing your relationship with the buyers, identifying what type of buyer they are and understanding their issues and perspectives.

It's also about using each of the templates I've given you in this book to develop the right proposition statements for this potential client. Take action to reduce the power and threat of any competitor, prove your competence, commitment and compatibility and produce commercial, well-priced proposals. Ultimately it's about giving your contacts the real confidence that you will deliver the results they want, on time and on budget.

TAKING THE 'FAST TRACK'
Have a look at the 'angles' for weighting the scales in your favour and maximising your chances of success in the Junction Eight summary actions over the page.

THE BUYER'S VIEW
'She knew that winning our business demanded her 100% commitment. But she also recognized that there needed to be some fun on the way – my team wanted someone they would enjoy working with.'

Get your moves on the sales journey right and you'll come over as a thoroughly professional person with integrity and drive. You'll also have built some great rapport along the way. You may not always win the assignment (life's not that simple) but you'll be able to pinpoint at what Junction you lost ground to your competitors, ended up marooned on the hard shoulder or even careered completely off the sales road. Such knowledge will leave you well positioned to navigate the next opportunity successfully.

GETTING INTO THE 'ZONE'

'He's the best I know at carving out small amounts of time to call people. That's why he seems to have never lost touch with a client contact. If he has a minute spare, you'll see him with his address book out, making a "catch up" call.'

Junction Eight: maximizing your chances of success

What is your contact thinking? What results will I get, and at what cost?

Your key questions and actions

Key question   Have I weighted the scales totally in my favour?

Ask them: 'Is there anything else we need to do to help you make your decision on the project?'

Test yourself: Have I …?
- Assessed where the decision maker is on the Relationship Triangle and what type of buyer they are (Chapter 3)?
- Put the right team forward?
- Won over the key decision makers and met their individual needs (see Chapter 6, Junction One and Chapter 13)?
- Really demonstrated my sector/specialist expertise and tailored my approach?

- Developed Value Statements and ideas the potential client has said will work and will set us apart (Chapter 6, Junction Three)?
- Outperformed my opposition in my contact with decision makers, and weakened their selling points (Chapter 6, Junction Four)?
- Used effective 'coaches' within the organization, and within the firm?
- Got the fee right?
- Highlighted the benefits of taking action now?
- Demonstrated that I am really hungry to win the work?
- Provided 'proof' through client references/demonstrations/testimonials?
- Demonstrated key products/services and benefits?
- Shown how we've done the work before (e.g. case studies as proof)?
- Checked the draft proposal document with key decision makers/coaches/sponsors?
- Kept in contact enough, and given the whole proposal 110% (Chapters 3 & 4)?

Act: Take corrective action on any of the above where you are unsure that you have done all that is required to weight the scales totally in your favour.

THE BUYER'S VIEW

'We want just three things from people we work with:

1 personal chemistry – get on with us, and value us as people and as a client

2 hard experience, with workable ideas – we don't want you learning on our job

3 reasonable costs – give us real added value, and we'll be willing to pay for it.'

So, there you have it, the connective sales route map broken down into manageable stages so that you know exactly what to do at each Junction. Every sales journey is different, but the principles remain the same. How good can you be at winning work now that you know the key things to do to reach your goal of a successful sale?

Let's focus next on an increasingly fierce battleground for winning new work in services and the 'big ticket' products arena – the competitive tender and personally pitching for the business.

GETTING INTO THE 'ZONE'

'Following my contacts from company to company has really been the secret of my success. Very few people stay forever in one organization. The knack is to maintain good relationships and to follow them when they move – it's very likely to be in the same sector or discipline – in which case, I can help.

'When contacts know you and trust you, they stick with you. I've followed one person into four different companies over the last 12 years, and he's probably not finished yet!'

CHAPTER 7

The connective way to win tenders

An invitation to propose for new work normally doesn't appear from thin air. It is usually as a result of your ongoing marketing effort, and there is no doubt that where you already have established relationships your chances of success in the proposal situation are greatly improved.

Those connectors who have experience of competitive tenders know that it involves much more than just producing a proposal document. Everything you do during meetings with your potential client and the relationship you build with them during the tender process significantly influence whether you win or lose the opportunity.

> Competing for new work in a tender situation is increasingly becoming the battleground for top professionals. It's a tough arena, where one mistake can cost you dearly, but it's where the experienced professionals shine because they know what to do, and how to do it.

The tender process brings out all the skills in their armoury. They need to showcase their abilities in the areas of:

- Rapport building and developing relationships
- Meetings management
- Written persuasion

- Questioning ... and listening
- Consultative sales technique
- Personally presenting their approach.

This section will take you step by step through the process, highlighting the techniques that work in developing relationships that win tenders. All proposals are different. The criteria for selecting the winner will vary from tender to tender. However, research has indicated that organizations generally have similar expectations, and in order to win it is important to excel in each of these areas.

What your buyers say...
Work with us ...
All organizations, when selecting business partners to work with, stress the need for them to be 'people they can do business with'. Whilst it's not possible to transform yourself into someone you are not, it is possible to use the connectors' techniques to improve your 'personal chemistry'.

Understand our business ...
Companies want advisers and suppliers who understand their issues, both within the industry and within their business. They have little time – or money – for people who don't demonstrate that they understand and, where possible, have answers to their problems and can help them to capitalize on opportunities. Face it; all of your competitors have broadly similar offerings – unless you have a unique niche. If you are not unique, then you need to make absolutely sure that your proposal demonstrates clearly how you will add value to them.

Give us your best price ...
Needless to say, in these days of tight budgetary control it is important in a competitive proposal situation to be acutely aware of the potential client's views on price as a deciding factor. Some sectors are particularly price sensitive and many

tenders are won on this basis alone. It is vital that your price represents true value for money. That's not to say that you should be the cheapest. Instead, it means that your prospective client will get the best because of the clear benefits that you bring.

> **THE BUYER'S VIEW – WHY DID THEY WIN?**
> 'The key things were the attitude of your people and your problem-solving approach. We knoew we could rely on you.'

There are three facets of a tender that, if correctly handled, will help you stand head and shoulders above your competitors.

1   Managing your proposal
You demonstrate your quality and efficiency during the research and relationship-building phases of the tender process. If you don't show enthusiasm, commitment and a professional approach to working with your potential client at this stage, why should they think it would be any different if you won the tender? How you build trust in your abilities is an important deciding factor in whether or not they choose you.

2   The written document
The written document reflects your commitment to your prospective client. A poorly written and badly designed document gives out all the wrong messages. The converse is also true. The ideal scenario is to produce a good-quality, well written and well designed document to add further weight to the relationship you have already built up during your meetings with your contact.

Your document can set you apart from your competitors. Writing in a style that is easily understood and highlights the benefits of your approach will make a significant difference to your chances of success. It is hard for a potential client to read three or more documents and compare them accurately. If your proposal gets to the point, and sets out all the information requested in a persuasive manner, you have a head start over your competitors going into any oral presentation.

3 The oral presentation

An oral presentation is often the deciding factor in the proposal process. The reason for this is that, generally, all of the key decision makers are present, and the oral presentation provides an opportunity to test the relationship between you and your potential client's management team. The connectors who differentiate themselves at this stage by highlighting the benefits of their approach, their skills and the value for money they bring, will score over those who don't have such a clear message.

A SHORT WALK THROUGH THE TENDER PROCESS

Picture the scene; you've been asked to tender for a big piece of work. What do you do now? Let's start at the very beginning … by asking yourself, do you really want it?

> Every new business lead requires some level of investment, and it's often a very significant one where competitive tenders for 'big ticket' work are concerned. Assessing your chances of winning the business is essential right from the start.

Experienced connectors take time to decide whether the business is going to be good for them.

Saying 'no' to a tender opportunity can be difficult, of course. The best way to draw a sensible conclusion is to step back from the euphoria of being asked to tender, to assess the real value of the opportunity. If the risks, attractiveness or financial return shout 'no' then for your own sake, and that of your organization's bank balance, turn it down.

How to politely say 'no'

The key is to respond fast and keep it simple. Ideally do it in person or over the phone, once you have formulated an acceptable reason to say 'no'. You could choose to respond in writing, and it may be less stressful to do it this way, but it also lacks the personal touch and may appear cold. So bear this in mind if you want to leave the door open to deal with the organization in the future. Take a tip from the top connectors and use a positive approach even if your answer to the invitation to tender is 'no'. If the assignment is not 'your scene' for any reason, or there is a conflict of interest, offer to refer the work to another organization you can trust, if that's an appropriate step.

Get 'in the know' before you go

Once they have decided to 'go for it', connectors know that good information on their prospective new client will help them impress their contacts and get the most from them. It's important in helping them to take the big decisions on how to win the work.

What to look for? An 8-point checklist (see Chapter 13 page 177 for a more detailed list)

1   What do they want?
2   What do they do?
3   Who's in charge?
4   What's on their agenda?
5   Whom do you know?
6   Whom do your competitors know?
7   What's likely to be the winning price?
8   Is working with them likely to cause you any problems?

How can you win your contact over?

Start thinking about what makes you and your business different and sets you apart from your competitors. How do you communicate your competitive advantage? It's all about making the most of the attributes you possess and then applying them in the tender process. The winner is NOT always the organization that, when all the facts are compared, looks the best – the prize goes to the professionals who can convince their contact that they are the best people for the job. There is a world of difference between perception and reality.

> **THE BUYER'S VIEW – WHY DID THEY WIN?**
> 'We were looking for people we could work with – people who proved they would deliver for us. The personal chemistry was right.'

Let's look at the 15 ways in which you can win your contact over and win that assignment:

Tender winner #1: Get off to a 'flying start' by knowing about them
There are lots of information sources you can use to help generate your initial ideas for competitive advantage. They'll give you an all-round view of your contact's business and a solid platform for analyzing its situation.

Even if they don't know the sector particularly well, top connectors have been known to amaze potential clients with their knowledge of the sector's key issues and the company's present position in relation to its competitors, all of which has been gleaned from studying the sources below for an hour or so. That's the power of using information properly, and often the difference between winning and losing the assignment or sale!

WINNING CONNECTORS DO THEIR HOMEWORK IN THESE FIVE AREAS

1   Analyze the company's Annual Report and Accounts. They will give you a treasure trove of information on the organization's priorities, mergers and acquisitions and the organizational structure, as well as on the personal beliefs and aspirations of top management.

2   Check out its Website and publications to gain a different view of its business, objectives and operations.

3   Dig up recent press coverage for latest happenings and opinions on the organization, its business and the industry in general.

4   Trawl through your own records to identify any past relationships with the company or your contacts, and your organization's experience in the industry. A dredging exercise like this often brings up other contacts of yours who may know the key contacts, or who have information that will be useful to you.

5   Get some 'insider info' on the sector. This is one of the best sources of identifying winning ideas. If you don't know your contact's industry well, read the trade magazines and industry reports. They can give valuable insights into current hot topics facing the industry and background to the market in general. They'll often compare the key players too. If you know anyone who works in the sector, ask them too. If your contact's organization is a public company check out the stockbrokers' reports; they can give you an invaluable insight into the company's market position and its strengths and weaknesses.

THE BUYER'S VIEW – WHY DID THEY WIN?

'It all came down to the quality of the ideas and the value you delivered. You were proactive and relevant.'

Tender winner #2: Be seen as a big thinker

No professional worth their salt wants to be regarded as not being 'strategic' in their view, by concentrating on the tactical areas and minutiae alone. The best ask themselves the question: 'How does my product/service fit into what the business is trying to do as a whole?' Do as they do by:

Looking 'top down'

Analyze the strengths, weaknesses, opportunities and threats faced by different parts of your contact's business. Looking at the business from a 'bird's eye' view will help you to see the big picture and talk at the strategic level.

Forming your view

Now identify all the products, services or areas of advice or contribution that may be relevant to your contact, including:

- Specific product/area of service required
- Capability and co-ordination needed
- Technical and industry expertise and experience.

Tender winner #3: Outwit your competitors

Your analysis of your competitors' strengths and weaknesses and your knowledge of their past tender tactics should help you identify potential approaches they may use. Champion connectors look for ways to develop new ideas to counteract their competitors' strengths and spotlight their weaknesses. They gain an edge by understanding specifically who the competition is, and what they are likely to be saying and doing to win the work.

THE BUYER'S VIEW – WHY DID THEY WIN?

'The personal chemistry between myself and your team was critical. You showed me that you were hungry for the business and keen to get going.'

Tender winner #4: 'Be there' for them

Analyzing individual contacts and identifying what they see as important is critical to your success. Put yourself through this test:

- What issues are at the top of your contacts' agenda to deal with?
- What challenges does the organization and the sector face?
- How can the business improve its competitive position?
- How can you help?

If you don't know the answers to these questions you've not done enough homework yet!

> **THE BUYER'S VIEW – WHY DID THEY LOSE?**
>
> 'You didn't listen to what you were told in our briefing meetings and the Invitation To Tender document.'

Tender winner #5: Get personal

Each of your decision maker contacts is likely to have slightly different priorities and preferred style of interaction. Your discussions with them should allow you to unearth the top five or so issues agreed as important by all (or almost all) of those contacts involved in the decision to give you the work. Try these for starters:

- What is each of your contacts trying to achieve (in their job or in their longer term career)?
- How can you help them meet their goals (corporate and personal)?
- What kind of approach do they want or need? (The answers to these two parts may differ.)
- How do they deal with their existing supplier/adviser?

Coming up with what you think are the major 'hot buttons' is only the beginning. Your challenge now is to introduce these into your future meetings with your contacts to 'test' if they really are the right ones.

THE BUYER'S VIEW – WHY DID THEY LOSE?

'You didn't speak to some of our people who were deciding for or against you – what do you think their verdict on you was?'

Tender winner #6: Show that your team works like a well-oiled machine

Your contact will be looking for your team (if you need one) to show that you work well together. Turning a collection of individuals into a cohesive team isn't easy, but it's essential. No contact wants to take on a team that has weak links and a lack of direction. Your key players need to demonstrate that they understand each other and the task in hand and have purpose, energy and enthusiasm.

THE BUYER'S VIEW – WHY DID THEY LOSE?

'You didn't come across as a team. It looked like a one man show to us.'

Tender winner #7: Ask yourself again – why will they choose me?

It's so important to keep your competitive advantage at the front of your mind that it's worth doing this scientifically. It's too late once the decision's gone against you to say that you didn't get your message across strongly enough. Get beyond vague promises into the reality of how you operate and what you will provide to your contacts. Set up opportunities to demonstrate the way you work and the value you give.

THE BUYER'S VIEW – WHY DID THEY LOSE?

'Your competitors already had a track record of delivering for us – you didn't show us that you were significantly better.'

Tender winner #8: Make a meeting a quality 'performance'

How well you come across at meetings and presentations is one of the best opportunities your contacts will have to judge if you are the right choice. Treating every face-to-face discussion as if it were a meeting with your most precious contact is the mark of the champion. Sending material and an agenda in advance, and thinking through their needs and how you can help, are the tactics of the work winners. They also know that quality of follow-up and the way they perform during the meeting will be where they can gain real advantage.

THE BUYER'S VIEW – WHY DID THEY WIN?

'The enthusiasm and intensity of your approach was the key. We were impressed by your dynamism.'

Tender winner #9: Put two heads together

'Brainstorming' with your key contacts can provide real opportunities to start working with them. Often this is something that existing suppliers or other competitors overlook. Get in there and suggest it first. But, a word of warning, the effectiveness of joint brainstorming sessions depends on five big factors:

- The quality of your preparation
- Your ability to involve your key contacts and their top people
- Your skills in running the brainstorming session
- The impressiveness of you and any of your people involved
- Your contact's view of the outcome.

A bad brainstorming session can lose you the assignment there and then. Make sure it enhances your chances, not blows them out of the water.

THE BUYER'S VIEW – WHY DID THEY WIN?

'The key to your success was a balanced team – no one dominated, no weak links. You all demonstrated that you could think on your feet and knew what you are doing.'

Tender winner #10: 'Haven't we come far?' Paint a picture of life after 2 years with you

Take a hypothetical journey through time with your contact and take a look back after (say) two years of working with them. What tangible things will have happened? What value have you added to them? How has your approach been markedly different to their existing suppliers?

THE BUYER'S VIEW – WHY DID THEY WIN?

'What you said was credible and practical. We could believe it, and see it happening.'

Tender winner #11: Convince them with proof

Prove that you have solved problems for contacts in a similar situation, show how you worked out the solutions and demonstrate the concrete benefits of your product or service. It helps them to understand how you created the opportunity or got to grips with the problem. Choose 'case studies' of people or organizations your contacts admire, and avoid any which may raise confidentiality or conflict issues. Where appropriate use the 'herd theory' (Chapter 5 and Junction Eight) to give them confidence that many other organizations just like them have already taken a similar step.

THE BUYER'S VIEW – WHY DID THEY LOSE?

'You relied too much on selling your products without understanding what we really needed.'

Tender winner #12: Benchmark them with their nearest competitors
Comparing them with their competitors can be a powerful way of getting the attention of your contact. What do they do better or worse in critical areas of their business? Demonstrate that you are interested in helping them to improve or stay on top. Everyone likes to see how they compare on key performance measures with those they are 'eye to eye' with in the market. Lots of on-line analyses are possible. Check out Mintel market reports, OneSource and, if they are a listed company, brokers' reports. Look at their trade press too – they often have a wealth of surveys, league tables and comparative information.

Tender winner #13: Get your clients to back you up
The 'thumbs up' from a satisfied client can provide a heavy-weight blow for you by building your credibility and that of your team. It can also highlight differences in approach between you and your competitors, and deliver the knockout punch you are looking for. People are often persuaded by quality third party support. But beware; it's vital to do three things before suggesting a client as a referee.

These precautions are not just common courtesy, they make sound business sense
1   Always ask your client contact if they are willing to act as a 'referee' for you.
2   Make sure that they are happy (preferably delighted) with your product/service.
3   Brief them properly on the key points you want to get across to your contact (otherwise they may concentrate on aspects of your product/service that were not relevant or important in this tender).

THE BUYER'S VIEW – WHY DID THEY WIN?

'Your price was right – it wasn't the lowest, but you demonstrated what more we would get for our money.'

Tender winner #14: 'Come up and see us sometime'

Bringing contacts to your offices can be an effective way of profiling your business and showcasing the resources and knowledge that will be at their disposal when they choose you. Stage-manage the visit to highlight key points of competitive advantage and provide the opportunity to introduce other key contacts. Demonstrate your interest and commitment to having them as a client – and don't be afraid to 'roll out the red carpet' and have them meet your chairman/chief executive if that's appropriate. Remember, such a visit must have a valid purpose, otherwise your contact may see it as a complete waste of their valuable time and you will go down in their estimation.

Tender winner #15: What does the place 'smell' like?

In addition to gleaning a vast amount of information from their conversations with contacts, the sharpest-eyed connectors will also have been on the look out for names in the potential client's visitors' book.

- Are the competition listed?
- Who is on their team?
- Who are they seeing?

Connectors will have their antennae out to get a feel for the atmosphere, culture, attitude and working practices of the organization – you can almost 'smell' it! And they'll also have homed in on their contact's office environment: the pictures on the wall, the books in the bookshelf – even the files on their desk – to help them get a feel for the real person they are dealing with.

THOUGHT-PROVOKING, INTERACTIVE AND MEMORABLE ... YOUR AGENDA FOR TENDER-WINNING MEETINGS

In the tender process, or at any time for that matter, your meetings are not just fact-finding missions, they are an important opportunity to develop rapport and trust with your contacts by demonstrating that you understand their business and their own position within it.

The meetings will also give you the chance to check their 'hot buttons' and test your ideas. If the meeting goes well you'll be building a working partnership by jointly exploring approaches to issues and opportunities.

> You need to make the most of every opportunity to build relationships and influence. To do so, you must be clear about what you want to achieve and prepare carefully. It means being flexible and observant during the meeting, and following up afterwards to create further contact opportunities.

So how do you make your meetings thought-provoking, interactive and, most of all, memorable? Use this connector's approach to think through the process.

Base your agenda around what makes you *different* and *attractive* to your contact so that you can test these in the meeting. It will show that you have done your homework. Think through ways that you can share insight and demonstrate that you know what you are talking about. Examples of where you have seen similar situations at other organizations, specific surveys, research, or observations you have on your contact's own situation can be real attention grabbers and give your credibility a shot in the arm.

Tender-winners plan in advance probing or 'high impact' questions they intend to ask, how they are going to get across the 'value' they can give, and how they will deal with potential questions or objections from their contact. Try these 'high level' questions for size. They'll demonstrate that you are a strategic thinker who understands business as well as your own specialism:

- What do you see as the major market trends/issues/ pressures just now?
- Are they likely to be different in the future ... how ... why?
- What do you see as the issues for your organization in dealing with these?
- How do you see the shape of your business in, say 5 years?
- What are your immediate objectives for the business, and what strategies are you adopting to get there?
- What is the current structure of your business/ departments/people/size/locations etc
- (How do you see this changing in the future?)
- What are your competitors doing that is affecting your business (and what strategies are you adopting to deal with these activities)?

There are plenty more questions of this type you could ask. They are intended to give you a good overall picture of the business' aspirations, hopes, challenges and issues. They provide a framework from which you can go deeper into the areas that are relevant to your own service or product. The 'killer' question to ask yourself is: 'How can what I offer really contribute to this contact and this organization?'

It's at this early stage where well thought-out and high quality material can have a big impact. This could include:

- Agendas – structured around your proposed approach, carefully worded and demonstrating thinking from your contact's point of view

- Team information – CV pages or a team 'card' giving details of your team
- Listing relevant clients (but watch out for potential conflicts!)
- Charts or diagrams to capture attention and act as a catalyst for discussion of key areas
- Appropriate publications.

Send any appropriate material in advance – but don't send too much. Swamping them looks like over-eagerness, coupled with lack of focus. Help your contact understand what you hope to achieve from the meeting and demonstrate how well you have prepared.

Many connectors use folders to demonstrate their professionalism and act as a reminder for their contact after the meeting. These may be either generic or specifically produced for their contact, supporting the theme of the pitch and the contact's culture. Some use the inside covers of folders to set out details of their team, including photographs. Think about how the material you leave behind contributes to the overall impression you make. You want your meeting to be memorable. Is the material you intend to leave behind going to do the job?

And back at base...

Top connectors know that prompt follow-up to their meetings is the key to success, and use this six-stage process:

1   **Capture** the key points, otherwise they, and you, will forget.
2   **Write** a personalized letter or email, thanking your contact for their time; clarify and confirm your understanding of the issues raised and the actions agreed. Send it as soon as possible after the meeting to show your proactivity and commitment.
3   **Prepare** tailored material on relevant points.

4 **Set up** any follow-up meetings or demonstrations, introducing colleagues if appropriate.

5 **Think** of ideas for other contact opportunities, which may include informal as well as formal activities.

6 **Assess** whether your meeting did, or didn't, achieve your objectives and why.

Face-to-face discussions are usually a critical element of winning big ticket work. It's vital to your success that you demonstrate your effectiveness both within meetings and in the actions before and after. Being proactive is an easy way to demonstrate that you are extremely competent and 'hungry' for the work – it can set you apart and create a gap between you and the opposition that they simply can't close.

WINNING 'SOUND BYTES'

- When we receive an invitation to tender we always make sure that our most senior person makes the call the same day – or the very next day at worst – to acknowledge receipt and, where appropriate, arrange to see the organization. We think this action alone sets us apart. We know from our market intelligence that in other organizations the tender is left until a few days before the deadline before someone gets round to putting some attention to it. They may even be more qualified to get the work, but by that stage we've been out there, met people and started to build some relationships. (Lawyer)

- Most people these days have a process in place for dealing with tender situations and, especially in the public sector, they can get really complex. The secret is to stick to the process. In my experience, too many professionals get sidetracked on other work, don't devote enough time to the tender, don't do the right thing at the right time and disadvantage themselves as a result. (Management consultant)

- Each point of contact with a potential client during the proposal process needs careful planning and execution. You start to create an impression from the first moment of contact. We know from past experience that expert handling of the apparently 'informal' elements can have a powerful effect on the final decision to appoint. (Property consultant)

- We focus on the 'touch points' where we come in contact with the client – and make sure that each of these is handled as best we can. I'm talking about responding quickly and effectively to the invitation to tender, preparing for any telephone calls, meetings and other communications such as emails and, of course, any formal briefing with the client, the submission as a written document and the oral presentation. All of these are where the client is making a decision about our suitability. (Process improvement consultant)

- The best thing we do with our bid is to ask ourselves, 'What do we have to do to win?' We do it as soon as we get the invitation to tender, and again after our initial meeting with the prospective client. Then we sit down and decide whether we are really going to go for it 'all guns blazing' or have little chance of success. It's a good way to identify a strategy for winning. (IT systems consultant)

- Where the client allows access to the key decision makers, we'll make sure that we'll focus our energies and efforts on meeting with them and understand their situation. The document is second to really trying to understand them and their business. At one time we used to pore over the detailed wording of the document so that we would get it absolutely 'right'. Now, our document is more like a playback of the discussions we've had and how we will be able to meet their needs. You can refine the document until you are blue in the face, but in my experience the extra 5% rarely makes the difference. I would rather spend the time talking with clients. (Accountant)

CHAPTER 8

Writing proposals that win work

Whether you are writing a letter, a report, an email or a full-blown proposal document, the basic principles of persuasion still hold fast. This section identifies the key elements of persuasion and great proposal writing. There's a real skill to it – but that skill can be easily learned if you know how to structure a winning document and write in a style that your readers will find enjoyable to read.

First, limit the points you want to make and pick the best, the ones of greatest importance to your readers. Your aim should be to make sure that your key messages stand out – so that your document conveys these even if it is only quickly scanned by your contact. This means, for example, putting your points in the order of importance to your contact. It shows that you know what is a priority for them. Unlike the miraculous wine at the wedding in Cana of Galilee, don't leave your best until last. Some of your contacts will have the attention span of a flea (or simply have no time) and won't get to your crescendo of a finishing point.

THE TOP BUSINESS WINNERS DO ALL THIS WHEN WRITING PROPOSALS

Identify the situation – summarizing the present problem, opportunity, complications and questions to be answered helps you to appear authoritative and understanding. This is just the image you want.

What results do they want? – set out clearly your understanding of what outcomes your contact is looking for. What results will they get from solving the problem or making the most of the opportunity. What would happen if they did nothing?

Explain how you can help – and why they should choose you. Setting out the options and evaluation criteria positions you in relation to others. Recommend specifically what your contact and other decision makers should do. And make sure that your recommendation links back to their needs and the results they want.

Highlight the benefits of taking action now – what's in it for them, and why should they buy? What difference will it make to them? When you've highlighted the benefits, go back and give them the 'so what?' test. Ask yourself if 'so what?' is likely to be your contact's reaction to each benefit you give. If so, strengthen your benefit by making it more relevant and tangible to them.

Provide the proof – show them the hard evidence that you can deliver on your promises, and that they can trust your advice. This is where you cover all the aspects of your proposal that show your credibility, competence and compatibility. What do they need to know, or have sight of, to convince them that you are the right choice? Think about including permutations of these: pricing and cost details, technical specifications, project plans, budgets, staffing quotas, delivery dates and milestones, Key Performance Indicators (KPIs), references, case studies, client lists and satisfaction surveys, positive comment on your services from reputable or public domain sources and so on. The choice is yours – just make sure that anything you include passes the 'so what?' test. What is your purpose in including this piece of information or support?

> The best mindset to adopt when you are writing a proposal document is to imagine that you are a journalist on a quality business newspaper like the *Financial Times*. Serious journalists are taught to write in a clear, easy-to-read style.

Even the 'heavyweight' quality press is easier to read than many a proposal I see. The writing is crisp, convincing and factual, with great structure. Journalists use a structural pattern called 'the funnel' that makes sure they start with the most important information in the story first, with supporting information much lower down towards the bottom of the story. Have a look at any newspaper and you'll see this style. You'll even see a mini 'executive summary' in the first paragraph or two. Here's how to copy them ...

The professional's writing toolbox
Write like a quality journalist – a ten–point action plan

1 **Grab your reader.** Messages unseen are messages unreceived. If your key points are submerged in fine print they neither persuade nor have the sense of urgency or conviction you want to get across to your contact.

2 **Make your arguments evident.** That means they must be simple, repeated, short and to the point.

3 **Write headlines that demand attention.** Five times as many people read headlines in advertisements as read the text underneath. Like all good advertising copywriters, get your promise, claim and main point into the headline, and reaffirm it in your opening paragraph.

4 **Use sub-headings liberally.** Sub-heads break up text, and summarize the main issue of the next section; cross-heads, as journalists call them, create curiosity and are carriers of your key points. If you don't believe their power, just look at any newspaper, quality or tabloid – they all use them.

5 **Use bullet points and numbers,** especially when listing a number of disparate points on a range of issues. Bullets round them up nicely, and give structure where there is none.

6 **Use 'concrete' words** rather than abstract ones, and avoid jargon like the plague, unless you are absolutely sure your readers will know what it means.

7 **Write 'actively.'** *Active* expression is more direct and forceful, uses fewer words, conveys energy and is more likely to conjure up a picture. For example, 'The building was destroyed by the storm' is weaker than 'The storm destroyed the building'.

8 **Check and check again.** Errors in typing, spelling, numbers, and grammar rightly or wrongly shout that the author is a sloppy thinker. A careless attitude towards small issues portrays a careless attitude towards bigger issues, and tarnishes what could be brilliant work. Get someone else to look over your work and make sure you use the computer's spell checker. No one has an excuse for poor grammar these days.

9 **Watch your face and appearance.** Writing at length in CAPITALS or *italics* makes for harder reading. If you are using small point size (below 10) you'd better send a magnifying glass as well. Very few people feel comfortable reading 'small print'. So, if you insist on it, prepare for your message to be ignored. Make sure also that the typeface you use reflects the nature of your organization and your message.

10 **Be clear, be brief.** Take the advice of the Plain English Campaign and keep your sentence length to 15–20 words, and use everyday English (e.g. words such as 'we' and 'you' rather than 'the insured', 'the applicant').

Make a great first impression

We know how important first impressions are in our social and business lives. It's exactly the same with proposals. Research has shown that the first sight of your document can have a really big impact on how you are perceived. It's critical to get the basics right, starting with the covering letter.

Your proposal's first point of impact is likely to be the covering letter and then the title page of your document. Don't lose the opportunity to make a real impact by using a generic letter and a 'boiler plate' cover.

Tailor your cover letters

Avoid tired old clichés and well-trodden paths in your cover letter. Don't use platitudes and redundant phrases like, 'Thank you for the opportunity to submit our proposal in relation to [whatever it is].' Such comments are just a waste of space – and are what everyone else says anyway. Differentiate yourself from the start by getting right to the point. How about something like:

'We enjoyed meeting with you last week and, as a result of our discussions, understand that you want to deal with the following issues in your business (list them) OR wish to focus on the following opportunities for your business (list them). Our proposal addresses these points and sets out how we can help you to achieve the results you are seeking.'

Again, at the end of your letter, don't fall into the trap of doing what most people do and close with the well-worn phrase, 'If you have any queries, please do not hesitate to call me.' Why on earth would your contact 'hesitate' to call you anyway! Apart from it being one of the tiredest of tired old clichés, this phrase puts the control of the next move directly into the hands of your contact – it's up to them whether to call you or not. Consider, instead, the line that retains control in your hands. How about: 'I will telephone you next week to get your views on our proposal and the appropriate next steps.' Use whatever writing style suits your contact, but whatever you do, retain control of the next move if you don't want your proposal to stall.

Give your proposal title some meaning

Most proposals I see just have the title 'Proposal' on them. Some go one better and say 'Proposal for…[whatever it is]'. Why not be a bit more creative? Think about what you are trying to do to help them, and then give your document a more relevant title – one that addresses the issue and gets some benefits in it too. Examples to give you the idea are:

- 'Improving employee motivation through a share ownership scheme'
- 'Developing improved management information'
- 'Communicating effectively throughout the organization through an intranet'
- 'Reducing your procurement costs by more effective purchasing'

You will be able to think of appropriate titles for all of the products and services you deliver which meet particular organizational and individual needs. If you are worried about being too racy with your titles, you could always fall back on the traditional 'Proposal for [whatever]' and then use your more racy title as a subtitle.

Make it eye-catching too

Pictures speak a thousand words, so they say, so if your document is becoming long, look for chances to replace text with a diagram or a chart. Good graphics can communicate information more easily – and interestingly – to a reader. Develop eye-catching headings or titles that reflect your key messages.

In tender situations the approach to be taken is sometimes stipulated, e.g. 'Your tender submission must be no more than 30 pages long and consist of …'. But even in these circumstances a well-structured and written document in a pleasing typeface will stand out from the crowd. If it's appropriate get some colour in there too. That's not to say you should make your document look like a rainbow. Picking out the headlines and sub-heads in a different colour is classy, as is producing any diagrams, photographs or other visual material. With modern computer technology all of these things can be done without fuss.

Test yourself

Getting the basics right

- Check that you have analyzed your contact's (and other decision makers') needs properly and creatively. Ask yourself, have I:
    - got a strategy that addresses these needs?
    - got all the information I need?
    - assessed the decision makers in relation to their: personality and style; level of knowledge and familiarity with the process; and their role in making the decision?
    - assessed my proposal for continuity and consistency?

Writing so that your words will be read and will persuade

- Check that your writing is crisp and concise – like a quality journalist's style. Ask yourself, have I:
    - engaged the reader with an interesting and tailored introduction?
    - used a natural, friendly tone and avoided clichés and jargon?
    - expressed myself clearly by cutting out all 'guff', 'flannel' and unnecessary detail?
    - emphasized and drawn attention to the 'big' messages?
    - demonstrated that I understand the subject thoroughly?

- made my sentences reasonably short, simple and readable?
- used words they would use?
- arranged my ideas in a logical and effective order?
- broken up blocks of text to provide 'readability'?
- supported my ideas with details and examples?

Getting the 'look and feel' right

- Check that the overall look and feel of the document is appropriate for the people who are reading it. Ask yourself, have I:
  - got the format right: A4, landscape/portrait, colour/ mono, glossy/economy? What will your decision makers want?
  - structured the whole document as if I was looking through the reader's eyes?
  - used appropriate graphics to illustrate my points and highlight my messages?
  - checked for silly typos and inconsistencies that will reflect badly on my attention to detail? (They will be in there somewhere!)

WINNING 'SOUND BYTES'

- We have a 'litmus test' that our document must be at least two thirds about them and only one third about us. Even when we are providing information about us it must be tailored specifically towards our client and their sector. It's a good way of ensuring that, when the document is read, there is no way that the decision maker could say that it's a generic proposal. We have been told that our approach is a marked contrast to some of the 'boiler plate' documents produced by other firms. In all honesty, we probably don't spend any longer on our document, we just adopt the principle that it should be about them, not us. (Lawyer)

- The biggest things we try to avoid in writing our document are tired clichés and phrases others will use. Everyone thinks they have the best, or most experienced team, have innovative ideas and are proactive, value for money and so on. If we include these things in our document (because they are genuinely true), we make sure that these assertions are fully justified, otherwise we'll be seen as no different from our competitors. (Actuary)

- We run an unusual 'slide rule' over our draft documents. We ask, 'Is this interesting to the client?' If in any doubt we leave it out. It's a good way to make sure that what we write is focused on what they want to hear. (Lawyer)

- We make sure that we hand deliver the proposal to our key decision maker contact, usually by our team leader. It shows our commitment to the work and says much more than a flowery covering letter. Of course, there are occasions when bids need to be submitted in a brown envelope and it doesn't matter who delivers them. Where it's unlikely to count, we don't do it. (Management consultant)

- We produce a very detailed plan of what we'll do in our first month with the client. It shows that we have really thought things through and gives them the comfort that we are action-orientated and ready to start. It brings a real tangibility to our proposal and shows that we are ready to 'get off the blocks' from day one. (Marketing consultant)

Whatever form your communication takes, it can be better than your competitors if you follow these guidelines. Tender winners recognize the importance of producing lively, interesting yet professionally written material. Give yourself the best chance of getting your message across by doing the same. Then you'll be in the best position you can be if you need to present your ideas orally too. And it's in the oral presentations where the business is often won or lost. What's the secret of winning? Let's have a look...

CHAPTER 9

The secrets of successful presentations

Organizations can sometimes spend thousands of pounds to get to the oral presentation stage of a tender. Often all their marketing efforts over months and years have been geared specifically to getting the opportunity to present, face-to-face, to the key contacts at a potential client company.

The ability to connect with those whose decision can have a sometimes life-changing effect on your future can't be understated. But why do some people succeed whilst others fail miserably?

> There's a lot of truth in the old adage 'It's not what you say, it's the way you say it', and this is particularly so when presenting. Even the most interesting topic can be rendered dull and lifeless by a poor delivery, but the reverse is also the case.

Even the driest of technical subjects can be made to sparkle if the presenter makes it relevant to their audience, and maintains interest through variety in presentation style, voice, pitch, gesture, visual aids and so on. That's what the connectors who win at presentations do, and I'll tell you their techniques here.

DO *YOU* ALWAYS DO THIS?

Whether it's an informal discussion or one with the backing of a full audio-visual production, the successful presenters ALWAYS do this: They ask themselves, 'What is my message?' and 'How best can I convey it?' These are simple but profound questions, and most presentation failures can be traced back to not fully addressing them.

Winning connectors know that their message MUST be memorable and thought-provoking; it must be pitched at the level of those listening, use the words they would use and be delivered at a pace of speech they will be comfortable with. Good presenters know that their body language will say as much as the words they utter – and they recognize that appropriate showmanship sets them apart from the 'also-rans'.

No matter what the subject, your audience – the board of directors, the purchasing team or an entire organization's employees – will want some common things; deliver them and your success is almost assured. What do they want?

THEY WANT TO BE:

- Impressed
- Convinced
- Reassured
- Informed

They also want to know what the benefits of your proposal are, what they will cost, the results they can expect, and when. That's the blueprint for any presentation, and the champs make theirs come to life. Here's how you can do the same:

Soothe your nerves by planning ahead

Everyone has nerves before an important presentation, and mulls over their words in their mind before they speak. But nerves, if not controlled, can ruin your delivery and spoil all your previous hard work in preparing for your big day. Luckily, there are lots of things you can do to reduce their effects. Consider these:

- Research your audience in advance and script your presentation accordingly. What do they really want to hear?
- Rehearse until you are familiar with your key points.
- Consider what you will do if things don't go to plan. Having a fall-back plan helps you to relax.
- Tell yourself that your potential client wants your presentation to succeed. They do – no wants to listen to a nervous or boring presenter!

You are not going to persuade your contact, or anyone on the decision-making team if you don't impress them. It's easy to 'miss the target' by not adopting some of the social protocols of presentations. It's also important that you use the skills of the experienced salesperson to make sure that your message has the greatest impact.

Many of the actions you need to take to get the potential client on your side are basic – and that's exactly the reason why many presenters forget them.

TAKING THE 'FAST TRACK'

Think back to the last time you spoke to a group and compare your approach against these 'best practice' tips:

- Note the seating position of the members of the potential client's management team, it can reveal a lot about the hierarchy. Act accordingly.
- Dress to mirror your potential client's style.
- Respect their territory; for example, don't move furniture without their permission.
- Acknowledge your potential client (and other members of their team involved) by name, and thank them for their time.
- Tell them how long your presentation will take, and stick to it.
- Use a speaking style that is relevant to them. Are they quick thinkers, analyzers, or other character types?
- Don't make claims without facts to back you up.
- Most important of all show enthusiasm. Enthusiasm is the single most important thing in a presentation. Show them that you believe in your ideas. If your presentation says nothing else, you will still beat any grey-faced opposition.

Come at it from their perspective

When presenting to the people who can say 'yes' or 'no' to your ideas, it's critical to see the issue as they see it. Don't waste your time trying to change the beliefs of your audience … instead, show how your ideas reinforce their attitudes. How do you know what their beliefs and attitudes are? Try these approaches:

- **Develop** an audience profile by researching the likely different levels of understanding of your services and what their objections and questions will probably be.
- **Identify** the sub-groups within the potential client's decision makers. Make sure that you understand and meet their different needs. For example, a chief executive is

likely to have a different perception and need of his/her service supplier from those of the operations, finance or IT directors. What are the differences, and how can you address them?

■ **Predict** the selling points your competitors will make and minimize them by making your own counterpoints.

Provide 'signposts'

'Tell them what you are going to tell them, tell them, and tell them what you've told them,' is good advice for any presenter.

Your audience needs some 'signposts' to help them get a feel for the material you are about to cover and to understand why it is important to them. Whilst this seems to be encouraging the speaker to go over the same ground and repeat themself, in practice this is not the case.

The introduction may only last a minute, but in that time the top presenter will have told the audience why the subject is important, why they should listen, what areas they'll cover and how they intend to present the material. In the bulk of the presentation they'll elaborate on these points and highlight key issues relevant to the audience. In the final summing up (again this may only be a couple of minutes) the professional, connective presenter brings it all together by recapping on the key message and explaining any actions the audience needs to take. It's a logical, easy and structured way to deliver a quality presentation.

Use empathy and proof to win them over

No matter how slick you are, you won't convince anyone without demonstrating that you have done your homework, see things as they do and are generally on their 'wavelength'.

People warm to people who are like them in what they say and do, and demonstrate their ability to get the results they are seeking. Show them how well you understand their problems by doing your research beforehand, in depth.

- Demonstrate how you meet their needs.
- Recognize the management and thinking style of your audience; make sure that your style fits.
- Use 'proof statements', examples, and case studies to bolster your credibility.

THE BUYER'S VIEW – WHY DID THEY LOSE?

'Your overall knowledge of the business was average, but no better than others – and you didn't demonstrate that you had gone out of your way to get "under the skin" of our organization.'

Detect the decision maker

Someone needs to say 'yes' to you and your ideas, and it's important to know who that person is. Too often presenters have been focused towards influencing the wrong person – someone who is not the ultimate decision maker. Why would they choose you if you have 'slighted' them by not recognizing their power or specific needs?

TAKING THE 'FAST TRACK'

Take a tip from the champion presenters and:

- Identify where the person who holds the purse strings is sitting.
- Make sure you cover what THEY want to hear.
- Influence them by showing due deference; address them by name; show that you respect their power by looking at them slightly more than the others.

Use the presenter's 'tricks of the trade' to build rapid rapport

You can't be a good presenter or make a superb presentation without creating rapport. Without it you can't develop the warmth you are seeking between yourself and your audience. There are some practical actions you can build into your repertoire to get that rapport going quickly.

- Maintain a gentle, non-confrontational, eye contact. If you feel more comfortable, look at your audience's shoulders or ears; it is less challenging than eye-to-eye, but still appears personal.
- Switch your eye contact continually between the group members.
- Address individuals periodically by name, where appropriate.
- Smile, and demonstrate enthusiasm – it's infectious!
- Use pauses and changes of pace to add texture to your presentation.
- Use your body language to best effect. Slow open gestures with palms towards the audience are positive; avoid brisk, jabbing gestures, closed fists, or chopping motions. Research has shown that these tend to make your audience angry.

If you really have to, use small cue cards rather than a script. A script makes it difficult to maintain eye contact and build rapport, and tends to indicate that you don't know your stuff... even when you do! Of course, the best way to demonstrate that you know what you are talking about is to have no notes at all.

Tailored, not 'off the peg'

An 'off the peg' standard presentation that contains generic messages intended for any client anywhere is not going to help you to win.

> Just as the high class tailor takes great pains to measure every conceivable distance and angle when you are being fitted for a 'tailor made' suit, so too does the top professional when preparing and presenting their material.

They ask themselves, 'How does what I'm saying relate specifically to my audience?' If it doesn't, they'll either tailor it to make it relevant, or leave it out.

THE BUYER'S VIEW – WHY DID THEY LOSE?

'You talked about your industry credentials and assumed you knew the answers – others showed a real interest in our business and highlighted how they could help.'

Create a compelling script

Facts alone aren't enough to persuade. You'll need to generate emotion in your audience, to 'paint a picture' of the benefits of you or your approach, and to get them to take some positive action. Keep your message short, snappy and credible:

TAKING THE 'FAST TRACK'

Talk about them and their situation. Be clear about what you want to change in the products/services to the potential client. (Unless you are already the supplier you must persuade them to change, and convince them of the benefits of your approach, otherwise you won't be successful.)

Your audience will have a short attention span (20 minutes maximum), so structure your script accordingly. Keep it punchy and packed with key messages. Add credibility to your opening remarks by explaining why you are qualified to make the presentation.

The evidence is clear, your Honour

We have all sat through enough courtroom dramas on television to know that what convinces the jury is evidence – hard, compelling evidence. It's the same in presentations. Whilst the greatest talker in the world can convince up to a point, the 'jury' (in this case, the decision-making panel) will want proof. That's why the experienced connector uses case studies of what has been successful before, references from relevant clients, demonstrations of how it will work, mock-ups, diagrams and anything else that says, 'This is evidence to show that I can deliver what I promise.'

Involve them

A 'talking head', someone who just stands up and presents, is easy to listen to for five minutes, harder for ten and can be downright boring after twenty! Whilst the presenter's skills are obviously important in keeping interest levels high, the longer they go on the more they are fighting an attribute of the human condition – attention span.

As the pace of business life gets faster, people become impatient far more quickly. (Ever get upset because your computer isn't processing quickly enough, or you are stuck in slow moving traffic?) So it is with presentations. The audience's minds can quickly wander. And the presenter knows that they need to keep them right there with them, not by talking, but by involving them. Asking rhetorical questions is one way, getting them involved in a demonstration or a discussion is another.

Assume the business

A common dilemma for connectors in tender presentations is whether or not to 'assume' winning the work. It is the difference between saying, '*If* we win the business we will …' and 'When we meet with you on a monthly basis, we will …'

'If' has the psychological effect of reinforcing any doubt in the decision maker's mind, so think positively and talk as if the decision makers have already given the work to you. You'll naturally then talk about 'when' rather than 'if'.

Make your visual aids a 'show stealer', not a prop

The decision whether or not to use visual aids is an individual one and depends largely on the material to be presented, the expectations of the potential client and even the dimensions of the room itself. If you do decide to use visual aids there are a number of options, each with their advantages and disadvantages (see below). The key points to bear in mind for successful use of visual aids are:

- Bring your own equipment ... you don't want the shock on the day of finding that the equipment doesn't work or is incompatible with your requirements.
- Put your potential client's name on the visuals; it tailors the presentation and shows that you have taken time to consider their needs.
- Make your visuals dynamic ... and readable.
- This is critical! Lay out the room so that your visuals can be seen. There is nothing worse than arriving to present your material and having to move the entire equipment or audience to make sure that they are in the right place to see your visuals. It's unprofessional and gets you off to a bad start, so make sure that you research the room first.
- Don't let your visuals dominate. They should support your key message, not be a poor substitute for them.

Choose the right horse for the right course

Any visual aid you use will have an effect on the type of presentation you give, the atmosphere in the room and how your message is received. There is no right and wrong answer, but don't just go blindly at it. Think about what you are trying to achieve, and in what environment, and act accordingly.

Computer graphics projector

Advantages: quick and easy to produce quality visuals and project them direct from your computer. Looks very professional and 'high tech'. Disadvantages: needs time (and expertise) to set up. Needs space to project onto a wall or screen. Possibility of major disaster if the computer fails in some way!

Overhead projector

Advantages: very familiar, everyone can use one. Can be used in a limited space, inexpensive to produce slides. Disadvantages: transparencies are not as professional as computer graphics.

Flipcharts

Advantages: can be used in a small space. Develops a 'hands on' feel to your presentation. Disadvantages: you need to able to write, and spell properly – and know what you want to say in advance. Difficult to maintain presentation flow and eye contact.

Desktop presenters

Advantages: easy to prepare and a useful low-tech visual device for very small audiences. Disadvantages: no use for any more than two or three people. Can be perceived as a 'salesperson's tool' by the potential client.

'Talking' book

Advantages: easily produced, low-tech visual device that gives structure to your presentation. Disadvantages: the audience tends to read the book or flip forward rather than listen to what you say.

The choice is yours; each visual device has its merits and its place. You may choose to use no visual aids at all or one that suits the recipient. The main point to bear in mind is that any visuals you use should be of the highest quality and reflect the standards you intend to provide; anything less will detract from your presentation.

Unleash the 'knockout punch' with a powerful close

We easily forget information given to us. (If you don't believe it, try to recall now what you read two pages ago – the chances are that you can't.) The best presenters know that it is crucial to encapsulate their key messages in a powerful closing statement, simply to make sure that their audience remembers them and their main points.

TAKING THE 'FAST TRACK'

■ Regain their attention. A long presentation has a tendency to 'lose' your audience.

■ Return to your opening theme.

■ Summarize your key ideas – five at most, ideally no more than three.

■ Re-establish your credibility to do the work.

■ Paint a picture of the advantages and future benefits they will enjoy.

■ Get some EMOTION in there, and thank them, genuinely, for their time.

Detect the silent message – what's their body language saying?

We've already seen the power of body language in rapport building. The ace connector knows how to read the non-verbal signs of his audience that say, 'Go on' or 'I'm not convinced', I'm bored' or, worst of all, 'You've no chance'. Be alert to body language that MAY give away the thoughts and views of your audience. Here are some of the obvious ones to look out for whilst you are presenting:

Leaning backwards on their chair, losing eye contact and reading their papers

You're in danger of losing them or you've said something they don't agree with. Top presenters will change tack on recognizing this by asking a question or involving their audience. The key is to halt a potential downward spiral and re-engage.

Your key decision maker folds his arms

It could mean that he/she is cold, uncomfortable with what you have just said, or simply isn't yet willing to be on your side. Experienced professionals know that this could be a signal for proof of their point, or a 'bugle call' to get the decision maker involved by asking them to do something physical – read a brochure, turn a page in the handout, come up to the flipchart etc.

Leaning toward you with upright posture

You've no need for me to tell you that this is someone who is eager to hear what you have to say, or at least is open to be persuaded on your point. You instinctively recognize the 'I'm interested' message – which is great news for you. That's not to say your job is done. Interested doesn't mean convinced – and convinced is what brings you success.

Don't forget the potential for using your own body language to achieve presentation success

You know the immense importance of appropriate eye contact and open gestures, and how critical the seating plan is in creating the right atmosphere in the room. Ace presenters borrow from the magician's toolkit to direct their audiences' attention. Just as the magic wand is a superb instrument for attracting people's gaze, so too is a pointer or even a pen for a presenter. Pointing at a visual aid, or a specific item in a report or presentation material, is a great way to gain – or regain – your audience's focus. Try it!

The presenter's toolkit – the do's and don'ts

Do ...

- **Save** your computer-based presentation on a disk or CD as a back up. We all know what happens with technology at the worst possible moments!
- **Stand** away from the visual aid as you talk.
- **Give** attendees time to read and digest what's on the screen (a good reason for not putting too much onto a slide).
- **Test** the equipment in plenty of time, and practise with it so that you can move from one visual aid to another confidently and effortlessly.
- **Use** a pointer if you need to refer to particular images (or figures) on your slide.
- **Turn** off the projector if you are speaking for some time without the use of a visual aid – or use a 'blank' slide with a colour that's restful on the eye.
- **Practise** 'handovers' with the previous and following speakers. Weak handovers show lack of preparation and look unprofessional.
- **Check** your slides for typing errors or wrong figures. People do spot them and lose concentration; in turn you lose some credibility. (Are you a person who lacks attention to detail?)

Don't ...

- **Turn** your back on the audience to refer to your visual aids – take a glance by all means, but keep facing the audience for the majority of the time.
- **Stand** in front of the screen. Have consideration too for the people at the side of the seminar room. You may be blocking their view.
- **Give** out handouts unless you want your audience to read them whilst you are presenting.

- **Rely** on anyone else to check that your slides are in the right order or that the equipment works ... it's you who will be in the spotlight if anything goes wrong, so be responsible for doing your own checks.
- **Brandish** a pointer unnecessarily, it distracts your audience.
- **Read** the words of the slide as part of your presentation – it bores the audience (they can all read). Instead, paraphrase, shorten and summarize the points, or draw attention to the key point. Get some life into it!
- **Have** too many slides. Each one must be of value in its own right, not just a poor 'prop' for you to remember what you want to say.

Presentations can often be the pinnacle of a connector's work with contacts. The skills are the same whether it is a job interview, a presentation to a board, or a 'pitch' for a new assignment. Being prepared, and seeing it from their perspective, are the twin keys to successfully 'dazzling them'.

WINNING 'SOUND BYTES'

- When you are presenting your 'pitch', you've got to watch out for signs of interest in a particular aspect, or the reverse situation, boredom and impatience. It means that you have to read people's body language and understand what's being said ... and what's not being said. Sometimes it is easier said than done, of course, when you are pitching to a panel. It's important to keep everyone included and avoid anyone feeling left out. (Advertising director)
- If we have the choice in any formal pitch situation we'll tend to go either first or last. If we do go first we'll ensure we keep our energy high and set 'traps' for our competition by raising questions in our presentation that the others will find difficulty in answering. Equally, when we are on last, our tactic is to be

---

energetic and different. The chances are that the panel will have seen a number of similar presentations so, by breaking the mould, we make a welcome change. People remember the last thing they heard much better than something in the middle anyway. (Accountant)

■ We try to match our audience in the way they dress and, equally importantly, their thinking and talking style. If they are quick thinkers and talkers we'll pitch our presentation in the same way. If they are more considered and deliberate we'll slow it down accordingly. (Advertising agency MD)

■ You've got to remember that a bid has to meet the needs of a variety of individuals who will be making the decision. You need to get into your presentation, not only 'the big picture' corporate issues, but also make sure you address where each person on the panel is coming from. (Corporate financier)

■ At one time, our people used to run a mile at the thought of rehearsing for oral presentations. They would simply have a brief chat through and hope it would be alright on the day. Their excuse was that 'rehearsals aren't like the real thing' or 'we'll be stale if we over-rehearse'. After we lost three in a row, and got feedback that our presentation style wasn't nearly as good as our competitors, we changed things. Now we insist on at least one, and up to three, rehearsals, the last being with an internal 'panel' to try to recreate the situation in the actual oral presentation. I must admit that all of our presentations – mine included – were awful in the early days, but now we've got much better, more disciplined and more practised – and it shows. Our success rate has shot up and we rarely get bad feedback on our performance. (Lawyer)

■ Many consultancies practise for their oral presentation and get themselves reasonably slick but, from experience of being on decision-making panels of a number of tenders, where people let themselves down is a lack of preparation for questions. I've seen presentations literally grind to a halt when someone has asked a question in mid-presentation and thrown the entire presenter's script off balance. Equally, it seems that some consultants simply don't prepare for obvious questions and get themselves tongue-tied as a result. (Management consultant)

- We've done everything in presentations from talking without notes in a 'fireside chat' style through PowerPoint slides to full multi-media presentations. I don't think this shows an inconsistent approach; rather the reverse. A multi-media presentation to the wrong audience is likely to leave you dead in the water; a cosy chat when people are expecting 'fireworks' is equally wrong. You've got to read your audience and, if you don't know what they want, ask them. (IT consultant)

- We make sure that, as well as preparing for the panel's questions, we also have some intelligent ones of our own. It looks bad if the chairman asks you if you have any questions and you don't. It's embarrassing and looks weak. A couple of good intelligent questions can help demonstrate our knowledge and grasp of their situation, as well as showing an intelligent interest. (Accountant)

CHAPTER 10

Overcoming the 'road blocks' in the sale ... objections

Once you've mastered the techniques of overcoming objections you'll be able to turn many of the ones you receive into building blocks for establishing stronger relationships. Hard to believe, but it's true. If you handle them properly many objections simply melt away – even the most difficult of all objections, 'Your price is too high'!

First, a few facts. Objections are part of our daily lives. We all make objections when we are buying something. Think back to the last time you bought a car or an item from a clothes shop. What words were the first thing out of your mouth when the salesperson asked if they could help? Most of us say, 'I'm just looking'. We *may* just be looking, but most of us enter a car showroom or a clothes shop with the intention of buying if we see something we like. It may not be an *immediate* purchase but we have been motivated to enter the premises for a particular reason. It's interesting, therefore, that we tend to protect ourselves immediately by saying that we are not in buying mode ... 'I'm just looking'.

We all object...

Creating barriers to the sale is a natural part of the selling process. Why? Because as a buyer you want to gather enough information to ensure you are making the right choice. Take your last house purchase as an example. Did you buy the first one you looked at without seeing any others? Very unlikely. The same could be true of the contacts you are talking to. They register objections because they want to *think* about what you have said, consider the alternatives, and make the right decision. Your contact will raise objections for a variety of reasons – sometimes they are not ready to buy, think they don't need what you are offering, or require further input from others.

Most professionals hate objections; they don't know how to handle them and see them as a 'road block' in the sales journey. It's helpful to change your perspective:

> See objections as opportunities to learn more about your contact's views and attitude. Objections can sometimes uncover a misunderstanding of what you are offering, or what you have said, and actually provide you with the chance to re-state your case.

PREPARATION IS THE SECRET

If objections are a natural part of the sale it makes sense to be prepared for them. Objections can be registered at any time in the sales process – from 'Don't bother me now, I'm just looking' through to 'I like it – but your price is too high'.

So, how do you create a process for turning a contact with an objection (or a number of objections) into a client? You do it through a series of questions that help to eliminate the objection, engage them in dialogue and determine what they want done. Remember, your contact isn't objecting to you personally, they're objecting to what you *represent* – and that could be change, your product or service, your ideas etc. Often, an objection is simply a symptom of resistance to change.

For most service providers it is reasonably easy to predict what objections are likely to be looming round the next 'sales zone' corner. The top 10 are listed on the next page. The key message here is that you can prepare your responses to these in advance so that you know exactly what to say to any particular objection.

The top 10 objections

1   You're too expensive for us.
2   It's not in the budget.
3   I'm happy with the service I get from my present supplier.
4   You are too large/too small for us.
5   You aren't on our panel of approved suppliers.
6   You don't seem to have the specialists/experience we need.
7   You advise other companies in our sector; we're worried about a conflict.
8   This is a critical stage for our business, I'd be concerned about changing suppliers now.
9   We've not used you before. How can we be sure you will be better than our existing supplier?
10 It would be too difficult to move our business to you (it will cause us significant 'hassle').

Many sellers forget the fundamental point that, just because you have a great product or service, it doesn't mean that your contact will see the value. Just as you have clients where you have worked hard over the years to gain a strong relationship, so have your competitors. Sometimes the sales process is a long one and you need to be patient ... your presence and ideas may represent significant change for your contact.

Your product or service may have a number of implications attached to it – for example, a need for training on a new system or, quite simply, the fact that your contact will have to break a habit if he or she chooses to work with a new provider.

Think back to your own feelings when you were asked to do something differently. Like the first time you had to use a new computer program. It was threatening, it was difficult – you may not have even been able to do the basics. You may even have given up and decided that the 'pain' of changing your habits wasn't worth the effort! Sometimes the changes that you as a seller represent have a similar effect on your clients.

(Now you can see why they might raise an objection or two.) It's the unknown, or the fear of the unknown, that you need to overcome. Your contact needs to be made to feel comfortable, and your job is to help them make the right decision by focusing on what's important to them, and the benefits they will gain by using you. Here's how you do it …

> It's vital to understand the thinking that has led to your contact's objections. That means asking questions of them, not focusing on how you can knock their argument down. The secret to objection handling is to keep the dialogue going by exploring the issues *surrounding* the objection.

Try this four-step process

1   **Neutralize** – by pausing, then aligning with your contact. This first step is critical. Pausing avoids a 'shooting from the hip' or a 'canned' response. It gives you time to think about what's been said and to formulate your move … which is to align yourself with them. You do this by agreeing with the *principle* of what's been said, but not the specific objection.

2   **Ask the right questions** – you need to understand your contact's reason for objecting, uncover what is behind the statement and link these to the goals your contact wants to achieve. Sometimes your contact will have hidden feelings about the situation – and the objection will be the result of these feelings. You need to find the cause … could it be uncertainty, fear, lack of 'need', worry about their own position, a vision of future 'hassle' … or something else?

3   **Resolve** – once you've got to the root of the objection, you're on the road to demonstrating your ability to solve it. If you've done steps 1 and 2 properly you'll have created some good dialogue and some insight into how best

to address your contact's concerns. Usually, objections fit into one of three categories.

a) **Misunderstanding** – your contact doesn't fully understand what your product/service will do for them (or you've explained it badly). The remedy here is to clarify what you are offering and how it will benefit them.

b) **Scepticism** – this is the objection that intangible service providers get a lot of. Basically you've not yet convinced your contact that you (or your service) will do what you say, or that your ideas and approach will give them the results they are looking for. Your response, therefore, must be full of tangible evidence – statistics, references, case studies, testimonials and the like that prove that you can do it, that your approach works – and it has worked for others in the past:

c) **Genuine** – we shouldn't forget that your contact may have a genuine point about some area of weakness in your offering. Put simply, they are identifying one or more areas where your product or service doesn't fit with their needs. The connector's way to deal with this is not to try to defend your weakness by arguing that your contact has it wrong. Rather, the technique of the champions is to demonstrate how the many advantages you offer significantly outweigh any disadvantages.

4 **Check ... and move on** – once you've given your answer to the objection you must verify your contact's acceptance of your response. If you don't, how will you know if you have convinced them? You've probably been in buying situations where you've raised an objection and received a response from the seller, who then just 'blindly' assumed that they had dealt with your point. You, on the other hand, remained unconvinced (and the sale was probably lost right there). If you are responding to an objection,

check your contact's attitude to your answer. If they remain unconvinced, you know that you need to clarify further or have more work to do in building the value of other areas of your offering.

You can resolve the 'your price is too high' objection with four questions

First, neutralize. You need to discover the true intent of your contact ... whether the price is really the issue. Say, 'Getting the best value is important. Can I ask you a few quick questions about our proposal?

1   After evaluating the options, is it fair to say that you like our offer?
2   As you were reviewing the options, do you feel that we have the best offer?
3   Throughout this process, do you feel that we have a complete understanding of your needs?
4   You've said that you are looking for a long term partner. Do you feel that we have the resources to serve you now, and in the long term?'

If you get an answer 'yes' to questions 1-4 ask the fifth question:

5   'It looks like you would like to deal with us, but we just have to find a way of making that happen by structuring our proposal so that it works for both parties. Is that right?'

If you get a 'no' to any of questions it indicates a weak area in your relationship or your product/service offering, and you need to either go back and revisit this, or consider whether, if you did lower your price, you would really get the work ... probably not.

Whilst objections can be seen as a 'road block' to the sale, they will always be present and, with the majority, it is possible to get round them if handled properly through careful preparation, professional questioning and a responsive approach to really understanding where your contact is 'coming from'. You won't necessarily overcome all objections, but your handling of them can gain you great respect and – here's the really interesting thing – you don't always have to resolve all objections to win the work – you just need to convince your contact that you are the best option!

CHAPTER 11

Nearly there ... negotiating profitable terms

One often-overlooked area of the sales journey is negotiating the final terms. It's not always the case that the price and approach you propose is accepted without question. Increasingly, in these days of tight cost control and corporate 'efficiency', you will come up against a situation where your contact has expressed a preference for your product or service, but wants to ensure that they really have got the best deal.

Let's face it, it's an awkward situation for a seller – the winning post is in sight and you've expended an awful lot of time and energy in getting to this stage, but this is where it can all go horribly wrong. If your contact is a much better negotiator than you it's even possible that you could lose money on the assignment. It's vital then that you keep in mind the whole premise of the book ...

> We and our clients share identical, mutual self-interests – we both want the same thing – a solution that truly meets their needs.

If we find ourselves 'boxed into a corner' we may end up with terms that mean that we cannot effectively give them a solution that truly meets their needs. As a result, dissatisfaction (on both sides) is just around the corner.

So, how can you help your contacts see that what you are proposing is truly in their best interests? Approaching any negotiation situation with this mindset immediately flags up your intention to obtain a 'win–win' result, so that you can indeed give your contact what they want and need. Let's have a look at this negotiation stuff and start with a working definition.

'NEGOTIATING' IS WHEN YOU AND YOUR CONTACT DISCUSS TERMS AND COME TO AN AGREEMENT THAT IS ACCEPTABLE TO BOTH OF YOU

If you don't do it well, be prepared for:

- Low margins
- Reduced profitability
- Working too hard for little return
- Unwanted precedents with your clients, making future negotiations and pricing difficult
- Weak competitive profile

Clearly, it's important to get it right! Let's explore some of the moves the experts make:

Watch the 'hidden' messages

If you observe sellers and potential clients together during a sales discussion, you'll see and hear 'messages' being sent by both, all the time. Your contacts infer things and make assumptions about you and your commercial position from what you say. For example, saying, 'Our rates are fixed at £1,300 per day' sends a completely different message than 'Our day rates are usually between £1,000 and £1,300'. As does, 'Oh yes, we can start straight away, we've got plenty of space in the diary', versus, 'Well, I'll need to check, but it might be possible to start almost immediately'. Your contact doesn't have to be an Einstein to work out what to do if they hear the former.

Avoid coming off at the 'first corner'

The 'amateur' mistake isn't failing to pick up important messages, or even sending the wrong ones; it's to start making concessions while you are still selling! Remember, negotiating is when you and your contact discuss terms and reach an agreement acceptable to both of you. It's about movement, and in negotiations *movement is inevitably away from your ideal outcome.* Your first mistake, then, is to start moving away (or sending messages that you'll be moving) before you've finished selling. That is, before you have taken your contact as far as possible towards your ideal outcome by heightening their perception of their needs – and the value of what you are offering. To put it crudely, don't try to win them over by conceding, or simply 'buying the business'.

'Mirroring' the best

If you want to be a top dog negotiator here's what you'll need to be:

- good at retaining facts and figures
- careful and painstaking
- constructive and trustworthy
- firm and fair
- quick on your feet.

Have a glance at the table below to see the benefits of doing this stuff.

Attribute	Why?	Benefits
Good grasp of facts and figures	You've planned extensively before the negotiation	You look professional, feel and act confidently, and take control appropriately
Careful/ painstaking	You seek to understand your contact's position You test viability of solutions	You discover what your contact wants, can identify flaws in others' arguments and get agreements that work for you both
Constructive	You seek proposals from your contact and show that you want to solve problems	You gain co-operation from your contact
Trustworthy (though not unquestionably trusting)	You stick to commitments and are open about how you feel about the negotiation. You seek clarity – and don't brush over misunderstandings Your behaviour is calm and controlled	You create a productive climate, and positive relationship
Firm but fair	You don't give ground easily and can challenge your contact's thinking non-aggressively	You lower the aspirations of your contact; are seen as personable, and definitely not adversarial
Quick on your feet	You consider 'everything is negotiable' and have worked out costs of any movement	You are quick to understand implications and suggest workable alternatives

Decide your strategy

An easy mistake you can make in negotiation is to give no real thought to what you are trying to achieve overall.

It's not enough to enter negotiations just 'trying to get a good price'. You need to know the wider objective of your negotiation.

Examples could be:

- To generate profitable business
- To develop long-term relationships
- To penetrate a new client or a new market
- To develop your own or your organization's expertise
- To gain an edge over your competition

Be absolutely clear about your underlying goals, otherwise you won't be able to plan what you say and how to behave.

Put yourself in your contact's shoes

Having thought hard about your own objective, start thinking about what your contact wants. It lets you consider 'where they are coming from' and will help you assess strengths and weaknesses of their position, highlight areas of common ground, and identify where you can get movement.

Take stock

So, you've thought about the strength of your position; you know what you want to achieve. Now you have to plan what to do to get there:

TAKING THE 'FAST TRACK'

You need to know ...

- What is negotiable
- The value to both parties of anything negotiated
- What will be difficult and what easy to get agreement on
- How you are going to use your preparation
- How you are going to behave

What is 'negotiable'?

You've probably heard the saying, 'Everything is negotiable'. Whether it's true or not, don't underestimate what can be negotiated. Don't restrict yourself to the usual few items – price, payment terms, time and delivery. Think about the structure of your work, the number of team members, contingent or success-related fees and so on.

Add up your 'currencies'

A currency is anything, tangible or intangible, you have that might be of value to your contact (and vice versa). Generating as long a list as possible helps because:

- It will mean you have as much flexibility (areas in which to trade) as possible, and will give you most room to negotiate.
- You are unlikely to be taken by surprise by your contact introducing a currency. If you've not previously thought about a currency, how will you know the cost of your making a concession, or the value of an offer from your contact?

Value what you are holding

Having thought about what currencies you have, now you need to identify how valuable each one is and, where you can, put a cash figure against it. For example, putting a figure on the cost of extra man-days, assessing the time-penalty of producing an extra report etc.

What will it cost to me to move?

Sounds like a question to an estate agent ... and you need the same level of discipline when you assess the cost of any movement you may make (and the value of any offer your contact may make). But don't only think in pounds and pence. It's often helpful to think in terms of percentages too – a 1% fee reduction requested by your contact might not sound much but could actually be a very significant sum. Or, to think in terms of precedent, any movement on one particular currency like hourly rates, or price per unit may tie you to that position forever. Hmm ...

Getting your act together

So far you've considered what you want to achieve, what's negotiable and your overall approach to the negotiation. You've also thought about your currencies and their value, and you've put yourself in your contact's shoes. All this is a lot of analysis and thought, and if you've got this far then you're much better prepared than most people entering a negotiation.

> The more you find out about your contact's position and needs, the more likely you are to discover tradable currencies that are high value to them and low cost to you.

No, I insist, after you ...

Now it's crunch time. One of you has to make the first move. Should it be you?

There will be times when you should try to be first with your proposition. For example, if you think your contact has unrealistic expectations, or where you have little flexibility to move. In situations like this you'll want to avoid the problem of having to move them from a position a long way from your 'negotiable zone'.

There will be other times when you have just no feel for what is acceptable to your contact. In this case you'll want to avoid making a proposal that leaves you so far apart that it's difficult to have a sensible and constructive discussion. In such a situation it's better for you to get your contact to make the first proposal.

Try this for starters ...

It's enough to keep you awake at night worrying about questions such as ... if you have to open the discussion how high will you start? How hard will you be with your opening offer? You want to show some flexibility ... but how much? What will be perceived as weakness, or arrogance?

The pro connectors adopt these advanced manoeuvres

- **Do** open above your 'hoped for' but not at a point that will blow your credibility.

- **Do** send a message about the degree of flexibility you have. If you have some flexibility (the usual situation) you should state your opening position 'conditionally' on other issues. If you have very little flexibility, you may be more inclined to state an opening position more baldly, or to add a commentary to the effect that you have little room for movement.

- **Do** keep in mind that the agreement is about the whole package. Make any provisional agreements conditional on a suitable settlement being reached on all the currencies. Suggesting this, in itself, sends an important message about your approach to the negotiation.

- **Don't** 'settle' all the 'easy' points first before raising the contentious ones. If you do that, you'll reduce your room for manoeuvre as the negotiation progresses and you might end up in deadlock or have to concede more than you planned on the major points.

Are you a lovely mover?

Negotiation is all about movement, so there are two things you will want to avoid – stalling and 'reversing' too far, too quickly from your ideal outcome. Here's how to move elegantly around the discussions:

TAKING THE 'FAST TRACK'

Pro connector's tips to avoid 'stalling'

Make your proposals conditional. A stark 'our terms are £1,500 per day' is more likely to stop the negotiation, than a conditional statement like, 'Assuming that we would be performing both the drawing up of the specification and selecting the supplier, we would charge £1,500 per day.'

Don't over-react to 'ridiculous' offers. Your contact may propose something that's simply not in the same ballpark as you. This may reflect poor planning or knowledge on their part or it could be a 'There's nothing to be lost' try-on. Dealing with this in a calm and professional manner (asking for reasons, for example) leaves the door open to take the discussion further.

Don't respond immediately with an offer of your own. If you do you'll come across as not properly considering their proposal.

If you've avoided 'stalling' you're on your way to a successful negotiation. Your destination is just around the corner, but watch out. If your contact is a good negotiator, they will know that now is the time when you are most likely to concede to their demands for a better price, more service, more time, or more people. You need to avoid going backwards from your goal.

TAKING THE 'FAST TRACK'

Pro connectors' tips to avoid reversing too far

Build the value of what you are offering. Make sure that your contact knows the *full* value of what you have to offer before you make a proposal. For some points – man days, frequency of meetings – ensure that your contact sees the costs and implications of *not* doing what you are proposing.

Don't concede without getting something in return. Whilst it's not always easy or possible to do this, or to get something equally valuable in return, it's surprising how often you can achieve it – and how 'generous' your contact can be when you have made a concession.

Beware as deadlines approach. There is a well-researched tendency for concessions to increase as deadlines approach. Establish the real significance of a deadline – sometimes it can be artificially imposed to increase pressure on you to give ground.

Negotiating is all about getting a 'win–win' situation for yourself and your buyer. You both need to feel 'ok' about the outcome, otherwise you will have trouble ahead. Remember throughout that at the very start of the sales journey you did a go/no go analysis on whether you should work with this client or not. You made a 'green light' decision that this was a client that would be good for you – but you also made an assumption that you would benefit from being associated with them.

The negotiation stage is a really good point to check your reasons for wanting this work. If it is to make a profit on the work, then make sure that your negotiation reflects this. If it is for some other reason, e.g. to enter a new market or gain market share, then check that what you are agreeing will help you to achieve the result you are looking for. Act accordingly.

CHAPTER 12

Are you a Rainmaker? (How good are you at winning new work?)

In the previous pages I've highlighted just some of the ways in which great business developers work to attract and retain clients. Maybe you can adopt some of them in your own business to make you more effective at winning work. Now it's your turn to look at yourself by comparing your work-winning behaviour and attitude with the best in the 'Rainmaker Survey' below.

There is no doubt that the ability of a professional to generate business for themselves and others within their organization is becoming a key personal attribute. Gone are the days where technical skills alone could guarantee a constant stream of work. In today's environment of ready access to specialized information locally, globally and sectorally, possession of technical knowledge is no longer a position of strength … potential clients see it as a 'given'.

> Those who are winning work for themselves, and for others within their business, have specific personal attributes that make them more likely to be successful. It's about doing the right things, at the right time, with the right people. It's about taking consistent, systematic action to put yourself in the best position to win new work.

The Rainmaker Survey, involving more than 400 questionnaire responses and 152 personal interviews with the best work winners from 150 professional services firms worldwide, has given me some real insights into what they actually DO, day-to-day, to bring in business. It's provided information against which you can benchmark your own approach – at both personal and organizational levels.

We're all different personalities operating in diverse markets and sectors, but the general rules of rainmaking still apply. The 'tick box' approach means that you can quickly answer the thought-provoking questions that will provide you with your personal 'rainmaking' profile.

How will you fare? Ten minutes is all it will take to benchmark yourself. What difference would it make to you and your organization if you could improve your own rainmaking skills by 10%; 20% ... or even 50%? What would happen if all your senior people could do the same?

THE RAINMAKER QUESTIONNAIRE

YOUR RAINMAKING STYLE
Which description best fits your personality type?
- Very extrovert
- Extrovert
- Average
- Introvert

How do you generate leads and win new work?
(Rank 1–5 in order of importance where 1 is most important)
- Contact making/networking
- Formal face-to-face meetings
- Cold-calling
- 'Farming' your personal network

Maximizing revenues from existing clients

Speaking engagements/presentations

Direct mail campaigns (including newsletters)

Seminars/workshops/exhibitions

PR/articles

Corporate entertaining

Other

ATTITUDE TO RAINMAKING

What is your attitude towards selling?

Dislike it   Don't mind it   Comfortable with it   Love it

What is your attitude towards serving existing clients?

Mundane   Don't mind it   Comfortable with it   Love it

What are the attributes which most contribute to your work-winning success?

(Rank 1–5 in order of importance where 1 is most important)

Optimism

Confidence

Persistence

Salesmanship

Specialist knowledge

Wide business experience

Energy/drive

Enthusiasm

Consulting skills

How much time do you allocate to business development in an average week (recognizing that you may be a 'full time' fee earner/client handler)?

5 days

4 days

3 days

2 days

1 day

Less than one day

COMMERCIALISM

How would you rate your technical skills in your area of specialism?

Poor   Below average   Average   Above average   Exceptional

How would you rate your general understanding of how businesses operate and succeed (in comparison with your best competitors)?

Poor   Below average   Average   Above average   Exceptional

What additional skills do you believe you need to elevate yourself to 'best rainmaker' status?

(Rank in order of importance)

Developing contacts/networking

Sales skills

Business awareness

Rapport building

Targeting

Greater understanding of client needs

Confidence/positive attitude to business development

Time management/delegation skills

Other

Specifically, how many sales leads* are you personally working on right now?

*tangible potential new work opportunities

0   5   10   15   20+   More

a) Was your last answer a guess?   YES   NO

b) Do you have your own *personal* sales lead tracking system?   **YES**   **NO**

c) Do you have a firm-wide one?   **YES**   **NO**

Do you, *personally*, have a system in place to allow you to have your contact's details readily available at your fingertips whenever you need them?   **YES**   **NO**

RELATIONSHIPS

How would you rate your overall communication skills, in comparison with others in your profession?

    Poor   Below average   Average   Above average   Exceptional

How close are you to being seen by your clients and other contacts in the market as being *the best* at what you do?

    Miles away!   Much more to do   Some more to do   I'm there!

Clients

    Miles away!   Much more to do   Some more to do   I'm there!

Other contacts

    Miles away!   Much more to do   Some more to do   I'm there!

What would you estimate the size of your network of 'good quality' contacts to be?*

*People whom you have previously met, who know you by name and would return an unsolicited telephone call from you.

    100 contacts

    250 contacts

    500 contacts

    750 contacts

    1,000 contacts

    2,000 contacts

How would you rate the strength of your relationship with potential work providers – compared with that of your competitors?

Much worse   Worse   The same   Better   Much better

How close are you to having strong connections with ALL the 'right people' in your sector (i.e. work givers, intermediaries and others with potential to refer work to you)?

Miles away!   Much more to do   Some more to do   I'm there!

PERSONAL PERFORMANCE

What would you estimate your conversion of sales leads (potential new work opportunities) into new business to be?

1 from 5 (1 piece of new work from 5 tangible leads)
1 from 10
1 from 20
1 from 50

Do you set a financial target for the amount of work you bring into the firm, as part of your formal objectives?

Yes
No

What proportion of competitive tenders (proposals) you are personally involved with do you convert into new work?

1 in 20   1 in 10   1 in 5   1 in 3   All of them!

How would you rate your oral presentation skills in proposal/tender situations, compared with your competitors/peers?

Much worse   Worse   About the same   Better   Exceptional

How would you rate your 'connective' selling skills in comparison with your peers and competitors?

Much worse   Worse   About the same   Better   Exceptional

On a scale of 1–10 how would you rate your senior colleagues' overall ability to bring in new work?

Poor   Needs improvement   Average   Good   Exceptional

YOUR WORK-WINNING BEHAVIOUR

Please circle one number for each of the questions below. The answer should best reflect the way you behave in your everyday business life. Look at the right-hand column first.

I rarely research an organization for the first meeting	1 2 3 4 5 6 7 8 9 10 11	I always research the prospective client (and contact) thoroughly before I meet them for the first time
I've not been trained in this area	1 2 3 4 5 6 7 8 9 10 11	I know best-practice proposal writing techniques – and I use them every time
I say/do what I think is right, based on my personal knowledge and experience of selling	1 2 3 4 5 6 7 8 9 10 11	I am excellent at getting my sales messages across in the form of benefits to my contacts
I am a poor presenter	1 2 3 4 5 6 7 8 9 10 11	In comparison with my peers (and competitors) I am an excellent presenter

I rarely look at the organization's 'big picture' strategy and situation

1 2 3 4 5 6 7 8 9 10 11

I always ask myself how my service/ product fits into what the organization as a whole is trying to do

I tend to concentrate on my offering rather than worry about competitors

1 2 3 4 5 6 7 8 9 10 11

I always consider my competitors' strengths and weaknesses when proposing for new work (even if they are not involved in the opportunity)

I get a good impression but don't usually formally think it through

1 2 3 4 5 6 7 8 9 10 11

I consider carefully the result each of my contacts wants (personally and organizationally) from my service product

If they raise it I'll explore options, but usually I assume we will deliver as we normally do

1 2 3 4 5 6 7 8 9 10 11

I always explore specifically the kind of approach my contact wants/needs

I usually front the work myself and sort out who does what internally

1 2 3 4 5 6 7 8 9 10 11

I invariably introduce key members of the service team to my contact

I reserve that intensity of approach for really important meetings	1 2 3 4 5 6 7 8 9 10 11	I treat every face-to-face discussion with a potential client as if it were a meeting with my most precious contact
No, I don't write so quickly, and could be better at thinking through the next relationship building steps	1 2 3 4 5 6 7 8 9 10 11	I write within a day of the meeting and ALWAYS look for opportunities to generate further contact
This isn't my normal practice (because ...)	1 2 3 4 5 6 7 8 9 10 11	I consider EVERY TIME how I can offer my contact a low risk 'taster' of my service/approach
I never use benchmarking, and I'm not sure where I would get the data anyway	1 2 3 4 5 6 7 8 9 10 11	I use benchmarking techniques to compare my contact's organization with their nearest competitor
I never use them	1 2 3 4 5 6 7 8 9 10 11	I use client references very frequently to back up my claims of results/service standards
This isn't my normal practice (because ...)	1 2 3 4 5 6 7 8 9 10 11	I invite prospective clients to our offices to meet our senior people/the team, and to see how we work

ARE YOU A GREAT RAINMAKER? COMPARE YOUR RESULTS

The survey looked at the characteristics of those individuals who were great at bringing in business for their organization. This section gives you an insight into what they are like – their personalities and attitudes – and what they actually do, day-to-day, to succeed in the 'Sales Zone.' The basic idea is that, once you know what others do, you can copy them.

The questionnaire above will help you take a 'snapshot' of your own 'sales zone' style.

- Which techniques could you build into your own repertoire?
- What can you learn about how others do it so that you can be more successful?
- How will you do things differently, now you know how the great business developers go about it?

What are they like?

The first, and most startling, conclusion was that 'Rainmakers' – those people who were great at bringing in new business for their organization – spanned the personality spectrum from very extrovert to introvert. Whilst we've all seen the 'hail-fellow-well-met' very extrovert sales person, most Rainmakers fell into the 'extrovert' and 'average' personality categories. However, for every 'very extrovert' personality there was an introvert.

Maybe the surprise is that introvert personality types could be very successful in the new business arena. My guess is that they are excellent listeners, and their thoughtful and consultative questions-based approach is what helps them to succeed, particularly in the advisory services such as consulting and the professions.

How do they get new work?
When asked how they generate leads and win new work, without a doubt those successful Rainmakers cited those activities that got them face-to-face with people as being most potent.

Whilst the order changed from individual to individual, the usual pecking order was:

1   Maximizing revenues from existing clients
2   Farming my personal network
3   Formal face-to-face meetings
4   Contact making and networking
5   Internal networking
6   Speaking engagements and presentations

However, there is no doubt that in the right circumstances – and in the right business arena – quality cold-calling is effective; so too are corporate entertaining, direct mail and PR as ways of maintaining contact and raising profile.

What do they believe?
In the area of attitude to selling, to be successful the survey suggests that you need at least to be 'comfortable' with it, and preferably 'love' the whole process of being in the 'Sales Zone.' Those who stated that they didn't mind it, or even disliked it, generally displayed less motivation to get in the 'zone' as often as they should, or a tendency to not go through the sales Junctions as robustly as is needed to be successful.

Do they keep it or pass it on?
Interestingly, when Rainmakers were asked about their attitude towards serving their existing clients/customers, there was a distinct range. For every one who got a real buzz out of serving existing clients once the sale had been made, there were others who found this aspect mundane. They thrived on the

thrill of winning the work and preferred to pass it to someone else to handle on a day-to-day basis. Neither approach is right or wrong. What's more, different sectors clearly required different approaches to serving clients/customers. Not everyone who wins a piece of work can easily 'hand it on' – the client has bought them, not someone else.

And the secret of success is …?

When asked what the ingredients of winning work were, most respondents highlighted their understanding of their clients' business and their skill in their specialist discipline, coupled with high levels of optimism, confidence, energy and drive – and last, but by no means least, persistence. The point to take away is that you need to understand your client's business and what you can bring to them *and* maintain your energy and enthusiasm throughout the stages of the 'Sales Zone'. Once your momentum drops the sale gets bogged down or disappears.

It takes time – but how much?

It was common for partners, directors, executives and senior managers in a business to spend two or more days a week on business development activities. Not surprisingly, those who said that they loved selling tended to spend more time at it than those who tolerated selling as part of their role. The key message though, is that, whether you spend one day a week or five at building business, it represents a significant investment of time and energy. So it's vital that you maximize your return by being the best that you can in your 'sales zone' performance.

I'm good, and I know it!

In the general area of 'commercialism' the best connectors thought highly of their own technical knowledge and skills, rating themselves 'above average' or 'exceptional' in all cases. And they thought that their general understanding of business was great too! Whilst there are cases where knowledge of business issues, how businesses are run and how they make money isn't important, there's a natural link between understanding what your contact is trying to do in their business, and your approach to providing the right support.

Keeping in touch, easily

Without a doubt, one of the key defining attributes of a great Rainmaker was that they kept track of the sales leads they had 'on the go' at any particular moment and had a lead tracking system that they used personally – often this was in addition to anything that their organization had. In other words, they had ownership of a system that provided them with easily obtainable information on their sales 'pipeline' and the status of each lead. Sometimes this was nothing more than a reminder in a diary – not all great Rainmakers went in for fancy recording systems. Invariably, all had an easy-to-access address book, either electronically- or paper-based, that allowed them to quickly reach those contacts they needed to speak to, or correspond with.

Being the 'go to' person

In terms of building relationships and general communication skills, most connectors saw themselves, unsurprisingly, as above average or even exceptional. Most felt that they were seen by their clients and other contacts in the market as being very good at what they did. Not all saw themselves as being *the best*, but nevertheless thought they were up there in the top echelons. Interestingly, this perception is important as reputation in the market goes a considerable way to building the respect and trust that business developers need in order to be more successful in the 'sales zone.'

Size matters – but so does strength

The size of a Rainmaker's network of good quality contacts depended very largely on the industry sector and type of work the individual was selling, coupled with their personality type. Those at the extrovert end of the scale tended to have, unsurprisingly, a larger range of contacts than their introvert counterparts. However, the *strength* of contacts was recognized by all as being an important factor. Most would prefer *quality* relationships with those in a position to buy, rather than spread themselves too thinly across a swathe of network contacts. Interestingly, very few felt that they had strong connections with *all* of the right people in their sectors.

It's a ratio business

The most fascinating area of the research looked into the conversion rates of sales opportunities into new business. Whilst much depended on the sector involved, it was not uncommon for conversion of leads into sales to be anything from 1 in 20 to 1in 5 or better. The implication is that it's important to pursue many to win a few … and to be systematic in your approach. The research also concluded that with better sales skills it is likely that conversion rates could be improved significantly.

Exactly the same findings applied to competitive tender situations where the average conversion was between 1 in 5 and 1 in 3. Again, the type of product/service being sold and the sector involved played a significant part, but there is no doubt that improved skills in tendering for new work, using the principles of the 'Sales Zone' model, were recognized as being particularly helpful.

It's how you say it

Whilst Rainmakers generally rated their presentation skills as being better than their competitors, this may be wishful thinking given the answer to the earlier question on the conversion rate of competitive tenders into new work. Whilst not all tenders require an oral presentation, in those that do, the oral presentation is a critical factor in a client deciding whether to trust you with their work.

It's all about the little things you do

In answer to the questions relating to day-to-day work winning behaviour, most Rainmakers featured on the right-hand side of the scale scored on average 7.5 out of 11. This means that there is room for improvement in each of those behaviours listed. These were selected by clients as the areas in which Rainmakers can differentiate themselves in the 'sales zone' by demonstrating their commitment, commerciality and capability throughout the process. Most of the actions are easy to undertake and it's simply a question of building them into your repertoire of things to do, and positive actions to take in the 'zone'.

CHAPTER 13

Connective selling – tools to help you

MAKING THE 'GREEN' OR 'RED LIGHT' DECISION

Do you really want this work – is it 'go' or 'no go'?

Attractiveness of potential client

(Place a tick in the relevant column)	Strongly Disagree	Disagree	Agree	Strongly Agree
Existing Relationship				
They are an existing client				
We have knowledge of the key decision makers				
We have good personal contact with them				
We have a good track record of past work				
Quality of client/ potential client				
Low risk of potential damage to the client through poor performance				
Clear requirements stated				
Good payment history				
No risk of insolvency				
Opportunities				
Potential for selling other products and services				

	Strongly Disagree	Disagree	Agree	Strongly Agree
Likely expansion of business				
Prestige in winning the business				
Platform to develop into a (new) business sector or expand our market share				
Likelihood of long-term relationship				
Competitive Advantage				
Competition is restricted				
Competitors have weaker relationships than us				
We have more, relevant, expertise than competitors				
We have other strengths competitors can't match				
We have the resources available				
We can meet the likely deadlines to complete the work/sale				
The sales process				
We have good knowledge of the selection criteria				
We understand the client's/potential client's needs				
There are good opportunities to meet decision makers				
Our contacts are committed to the process				
Totals				

WHAT TYPE OF BUYER ARE THEY?

Economic buyers

Typical characteristics

Look for price performance, value for money, return on investment

Responsible for bottom line impact on the organization

Give final 'Yes' or 'No'

Roles in the sale

Take the decision to go out to tender/ buy and assess who should be on the list and the decision criteria

Decide on the process and manage it

Make the final decision

User buyers

Typical characteristics

Look for impact on job performance and efficiency

Will work with your products/people on a day-to-day basis

Their personal success is linked to your product or service, so they will judge subjectively

Roles in the sale

Assess you subjectively during meetings and provide feedback

Compare competitor's propositions subjectively and provide feedback

Technical buyers

Typical characteristics

Look for measurable, quantifiable aspects of each pitch

Focus on the product or service itself – does it meet the detailed specification?

Screen out organizations on the basis of technicalities; can give final 'No'

Make recommendations

Roles in the sale

Assess propositions for technical content

Observe each organization's conduct and performance objectively during the sales process

Look at each organization's proposals objectively and provide feedback

IDENTIFYING YOUR COACHES, SPONSORS AND ANTI-SPONSORS

Coaches	Sponsors	Anti-Sponsors
Typical characteristics	**Typical characteristics**	**Typical characteristics**
Have credibility and influence with the buyers	Have credibility and influence with the buyers	Have credibility and influence with the buyers
You have credibility with them	Support you and your people, and want you to be selected	Want you out, or not selected
Support you and want you to succeed	Likely to have been involved with you in the past	Perceive you as a threat
Roles in the sale		Act as sponsor for your opposition
Provide tactical guidance on:	See their own self interests served by the development of a relationship between you and the buyers	May have internal conflict with your sponsors or coaches
Buyers' roles, power bases and personal wins		Your appointment may be a personal loss to them
Your proposition and people selection – they know how you are perceived as individuals and as an organization	**Roles in the sale**	**Roles in the sale**
Know the pricing 'ball park'	Carry weight in decision-making process	Carry weight in decision-making process
Alert you to opposition manoeuvres	Have impact on how you are perceived	Want to undermine your efforts
Have access to additional background information on the prospect, the decision-making process and shifts in decision criteria	Underwrite and endorse you and your propositions	Underwrite and endorse the opposition
Help you position yourself with each buyer	Can give you public support	
Have regular informal contact with you		

DECISION MAKERS – ANALYSIS TOOL

Contact name:

What are they like?	How important to the sale are they?	Attitude to you/ your business?

Consider:

Personality, management style, business, education and social background; likes and dislikes.

What kind of buyer are they: Technical, Economic or User?

Consider:

Key decision-maker or not? Relationships with other buyers (stronger or weaker)

Level of respect within the business

Consider:

Likely sponsor, anti-sponsor, coach or neutral?

Will they favour you or not?

Results Required

Business	Personal

Consider:

What do they want for the business?
What do they want to achieve personally?
What personal 'wins' would there be by choosing you?
(Think kudos, promotion, safety, respect, problem removal, 'easier life' etc)

DECISION MAKERS – ACTION TOOL

Contact name:

**Influencing your
contact's attitude**

Action options: formal and informal meetings, discussions, telephone calls, letters, emails, product/service demos, invitations to your office/sites, corporate hospitality, use of coaches and sponsors to influence, research into specific areas of interest/concern, potential short (free?) assignments to influence opinion and demonstrate your working style. Think creatively about what devices you can use to change a neutral or negative attitude to a positive one.

**The Action Route Map
– what key actions will you take, and when?**

What do they think of you? (Very positive is a 10, very negative is a 1.) How does their attitude change over time?

Month one

Month two

Month three

Month four

Month five

Month six

Month seven

COMPETITORS – MAPPING TOOL

Who are they?

Starting Grid:
Competitors' existing relationships and product/service offerings

Consider:	Competitors' strengths	Competitors' weaknesses
Reputation with this organisation and in this sector; experience of this type of assignment		

Starting Grid Ranking
Your position relative to your competitors (1st/2nd etc)

Manoeuvres: What will they be doing to win the work?

Likely competitor tactics	Your actions to counteract competitor strengths and highlight weaknesses

Overtaking Update
Have you improved your position through the actions you have taken?

VALUE STATEMENT TOOL

The Decision Maker

Who
Who is the decision maker? (Name and position at the potential client)
Your value statement needs to be tailored specifically to each of the decision makers

Issues
What are the potential client's issues and opportunities?
These need to be recognised by the decision maker as being important to them

How will the issues and opportunities affect each decision maker?
What are the implications of not taking action?
What benefits will they get if they do?

Need
What result does the decision maker want?
(e.g. make money/reduce risk/increase efficiency/comply with legislation/beat competition etc.)

Objections
Will what you propose really work – and what are the financial/risk/credibility/disruption/cost implications?

Your offer

Product/Service
Offering
How does my chosen solution address the decision maker's issues and opportunities, respond to their needs and deal with any worries or objections they may have?

Differentiation
Why choose me?
What product/service/solution/approach, references, previous experience, credentials etc. will set me apart from my competitors?

Results

Value added
What tangible, financial and measurable results will they get?

My Value Statement
Using the above answers, develop a statement which effectively answers the questions why should this buyer buy this product or service from you

MAKING SALES MEETINGS WORK – PRE- AND POST-MEETING TOOLS

Pre-meeting tool

Who will be there?	Decision makers to be present
What do you/they want to cover?	Key points for each buyer (from my Decision Makers Analysis)
How will I approach their issues and opportunities?	Agenda points
How can I convince them?	Examples, case studies, research and credentials I can use
How will I respond to their questions?	Their likely questions and potential objections
Should I take anyone else with me?	My attendees and what they will say and do
Meeting	How will I gain an edge over the competition?

Post-meeting tool

Meeting	Prepare meeting notes and highlight key points of information
Share the result	Include key points and agreed actions in follow-up communication to decision maker(s)
Check on your performance	Obtain feedback on the meeting from the decision makers (and/or coach/sponsor)
Update your position	Update your Decision Makers Analysis
Deliver on your promises	Other actions I need to take

A CONTACT MAP FOR INDIVIDUAL DECISION MAKERS

Decision Makers	Week 1	Week 2	Week 3
Commercial Director	• Call to confirm meeting and ask for input to agenda • Email the agenda in advance of the meeting • Letter covering key points of the meeting and agreed actions	• Email to confirm second meeting • Meeting to discuss outcome of demo and our research into particular issues • Follow-up letter focusing on key actions	• Deliver proposal document • Follow-up call for views, and queries
IT Director	• Arrange informal lunch with me and colleagues	• Demonstrate the new product/service • Follow-up call to assess reactions to the demo	• Deliver proposal document • Make followup call
Chief Executive	• Set up demo of our product/service	• Send agenda for product/service demo • Meeting, followed by letter highlighting key points	• Deliver proposal document • Followup call to check progress and confirm decision-making process

Further reading

Alessandra, T. and Barrera, R. *Collaborative Selling, How to Gain the Competitive Edge in Sales* (John Wiley & Sons 1993)

Barnes, James G. *Secrets of Customer Relationship Management* (McGraw Hill 2001)

Bosworth, Michael T. *Solution Selling* (Irwin 1995)

Bowman, Lee *High Impact Business Presentations* (Century Business 1993)

Freese, Thomas A. *Secrets of Questions-Based Selling* (Sourcebooks 2000)

Heiman, Stephen E. *et al. The New Strategic Selling* (Kogan Page 1998)

Hopkins, Tom *Selling for Dummies* (IDG Books Worldwide 1995)

Khalsa, Mahan *Let's Get Real or Let's Not Play* (Franklin Covey 1999)

Leeds, Dorothy *Powerspeak* (Piatkus Books 1988)

Lewis, David *The Secret Language of Success* (Corgi 1990)

Lewis, Dr David *Winning New Business: A Practical Guide to Successful Sales Presentations* (Piatkus Books 1993)

Maister, David H. *Practice What You Preach* (The Free Press 2001)

Maister, David H. *The Trusted Adviser* (The Free Press 2002)

McKay, Harvey *Swim With the Sharks Without Being Eaten Alive* (W M Morrow & Co Inc 1988)

Parinello, Anthony *Selling to VITO (the Very Important Top Officer)* (Adams Media Corporation 1999)

Pease, Allan *Body Language: How to Read Others' Thoughts by Their Gestures* (Sheldon Press 1997)

Peoples, David *Selling to the Top* (Wiley 1993)

Rackham, Nigel *Spin Selling* (McGraw Hill 1988)

Roe, Michael *Marketing Professional Services: Winning New Business in the Professional Services Sector* (Butterworth-Heinemann 1998)

Roe, Michael *Marketing Professional Services: Winning New Business in the Professional Services Sector* (Butterworth-Heinemann 2001)

Sant, Tom *Persuasive Business Proposals* (Amacom 1992)

Smith, P.R. with Taylor, Jonathan *Marketing Communications* (Kogan Page 2002)

Spencer Johnson M.D. *The One Minute Salesperson* (Fontana/Collins 1988)

Tasso, Kim *Selling Skills for Professionals* (Hawksmere 1999)

Timperley, John *Network Your Way to Success* (Piatkus Books 2002)

Washburn, Harry and Wallace, Kim *Why People Don't Buy Things* (Perseus 2000)

Audio tapes

Brennan, Charles Jnr *Advanced Consultative Selling* (Brennan Sales Institute)

Sandler, David *Close the Deal: The Sandler Sales Institute's Seven Step System of Successful Selling* (Nightingale Conant)

Index